The Legend of 'THE NINE'

Some of the names of the people in this true story have been changed in order to protect their privacy.

All rights reserved. No part of this book may be reproduced or transmitted in any form or by any means, electronic or mechanical, including photocopying, recordings, audio, video or by any information storage and retrieval system, or any form whatsoever without permission in writing from Jenna Orion.

Library of Congress Cataloging-in-Publication Data
Orion, Jenna

The Legend of 'The Nine': The Untold Story
Orion, Jenna

www.jennaorion.com
Universal Changes, Inc.
Printed in the United States of America

Copyright © 2010 Jenna Orion
All rights reserved.

ISBN: 1-4537-1246-1
ISBN-13: 9781453712467

The Legend of 'THE NINE'

The Untold Story

Jenna Orion

CONTENTS

ACKNOWLEDGMENTS ix
PREFACE xi

1. Space Travelers Visit Orlando 1
2. Electrical Encounters of the Earthly Kind 17
3. Chance or Fate? 25
4. Visitors, Earth Changes, and Reincarnation 33
5. Ask and You Shall Receive 63
6. Aborted 77
7. It's Space Mountain Time 89
8. The Star in the East: Mystery Solved 115
9. Witnesses 141
10. Beamed Up? 169
11. The Plot Thickens 187
12. Reverse Polarity 195
13. Restructuring 199
14. X-Ray Vision 211
15. Living Between Worlds and Near Death Experience 217
16. Life Before Birth 233

**Cover artwork by Will Bueche',
based on the original illustration by Tom White**

The artwork depicts one of the spacecraft I was fortunate enough to encounter. This incident was near Clearwater Beach, Florida.

The depiction of the craft is identical to what I saw, except for the number of small circles of lights on its bottom and their proximity to its outer edge.

The circle of lights in the upper, right-hand corner of the artwork represents the huge number of spacecrafts that circled out over the ocean at a great distance. They accompanied the spacecraft pictured in the lower part of the artwork.

Acknowledgments

Thanks to my companions, the Ascended Masters and The Nine, who are the true authors of this book. Without Them, I would have been alone in creating it. I also wish to thank Them for Their continual, diligent work to improve the entire Universe.

I also wish to acknowledge the late John E. Mack, MD, professor at Harvard, Pulitzer Prize winner, author of *Abduction* and renowned hypnotic regression expert. I am grateful for his service to me as well as to humanity and our advancement into a new reality. Without him, I may not have had the courage to go public with my life's story. He kept in touch and was always there for me on a moment's notice. He had a brilliant mind and an ability to perform professional regressions. I still cannot grasp the fact that he is gone from Earth. I miss him and the gift that he shared so generously with all of us. I will always be grateful for the work he did on Earth; his death is a great loss for me, for all who knew him, and a great loss for humanity.

I would like to give special thanks to my daughter for being my best friend throughout life. Let me give very special thanks to those who have passed on for their contribution to this book after their deaths, especially to my mother and father. In life, my father was always a great provider for his family. My mother was the best mother in the world; her entire life was spent in service to her family and God.

I also want to give thanks to Rebecca Gomez Farrell, who stepped in after the creation of the book to give her expertise at dotting the i's and crossing the t's. Thanks to my friends Sue, Paula, Pam, and Paul, who have given me moral support. Last but not least, thanks to my friend Laurie Hannan Anton, who continued to challenge me to pursue my mission of writing this book. As an entertainment attorney, she was also there to assist when I needed advice.

Preface

This book is the true story of my life, as well as the true story of The Nine. It details many of the bizarre encounters I have had in this lifetime. These encounters are ongoing and have been with several different groups of Beings who come to Earth in spacecraft. They have been varied in intent; however, the majority of the book is about the most meaningful and purposeful encounters I have had with a group of Omniscient human Light Beings I refer to as The Nine. They are as human as we are, yet these Beings possess a God-like power that is beyond belief. These Enlightened Beings work hand in hand with Ascended Masters who have also been guiding me throughout my life. Their goal is to bring enlightening messages to Earth through me as Their spokesperson. The Nine leave nothing to the imagination, including the fact that They truly are Messengers from God and coauthors of this book.

Their enlightening messages are meant to bring us information about our future, as well as to rid the false reality that most of us live in.

This book also tells of additional fascinating and inspiring spiritual events that I have experienced in this lifetime. These experiences were very meaningful for me and teach the same lessons to all of us. They include my near-death experience, spiritual healings, restructuring of my body, gaining an enhanced soul, learning of and living parallel and simultaneous lives, X-ray vision, and visits with friends and family after their deaths, both here and on the other side.

These experiences, when viewed together, have created an *inspiring* and *positive* story that plays out much like the movie *Field of Dreams* times ten because it also had endless, seemingly coincidental events that were far too numerous to be coincidental. As it turned out in the film and in my life, these coincidences were nothing more than fate.

The plot thickens when I recount how the God-like Beings orchestrated a meeting for me with Doctor Mack. Through my work with Doctor Mack, I uncovered shocking revelations that will be very intriguing and illuminating for the people of Earth.

Here's hoping you will read this book with an open mind and take from it the information that rings true to you. I also hope that you have as many Aha! moments as I have had and that you gain a new view of reality that makes a lot more sense than the one you previously had. Most importantly, I hope this book brings faith back to those who have lost even a small portion of it, as that is the Enlightened Beings' and my intended purpose for it. This book is only a small part of my destined mission; however, it is a very important one.

Chapter 1
Space Travelers Visit Orlando

I now know beyond a shadow of a doubt that there really is life on other planets. I also know beyond a shadow of a doubt that I am here on Earth to carry out and complete a specific mission.

In this lifetime, I have had endless alien encounters. Since these encounters began, I have had contact with several different alien species. The first are a group of very tall, human Light Beings with a loving, God-like spiritual energy. They have sturdy physiques and are unbelievably humanlike in every way. They are *The* Nine and say They are Messengers from God. They are extremely powerful and enlightened spiritually. There is also a large group of regal-looking humanoids who all appear identical, as if cloned. I have also had an encounter with an *Intruder* who wore a hooded garment that overshadowed his face, and encounters with the *Zetas*, or *short Greys*, whom you won't be reading much about in this book.

I have also had lifelong visits with various *Ascended Masters*. These entities work hand in hand with The Nine. Collectively, They are my Guides.

In reality, these Messengers are not aliens. Some may call Them *Humanoid*, because we earthlings are so programmed to use the term humanoids to describe those who come to Earth in spacecraft. I know the Messengers very well and understand just how human They really are, therefore I prefer not to refer to Them as humanoid. I respect who They are as enlightened humans and Messengers from God.

These Messengers have different appearances and varied universalities that give each of Them Their own identity just like we have different appearances and varied nationalities that make us individuals. Their physical appearances are basically no different from ours. What sets Them apart from us is Their extremely high vibrational frequency, Their omniscience that allows Them to know the answers to everything that is, and Their extreme power that is beyond belief.

My visits with Them have been extremely positive and rewarding, although bizarre by human standards. These same Messengers and the Ascended Masters have been my constant companions throughout life. I want to share with you the true purpose of my encounters with Them and Their Teachings. These Teachings are very enlightening and were telepathically dictated to me.

These visits have allowed me a glimpse into the future of Planet Earth. In addition, many of the mysteries of the ages have been solved for me through the information They have shared. These are facts that have been kept secret and omitted from the Bible, therefore giving the world a distorted view of things, *a false reality*. A number of these secrets from the Messengers are revealed throughout this book, per Their instructions.

You will soon learn from this book that there are many varieties of life-forms visiting Earth. I have heard various accounts of other people who've had alien encounters, but so far, I have never heard of an encounter like mine with the Messengers.

My life is different from most people's because I have always had continual guidance from my collective Guides. In my earlier years, I thought that guidance from Them was the *normal* way of life and didn't question who They were. I have since learned some of the names of these Guides who have been impeccably guiding me down my life's path.

I often feel very alone, because I haven't found any common ground with other *experiencers*—others who have had alien encounters. Some are similar in a vague way, but none of them are really like mine. Although I have had innumerable, in-person visits with the Messengers who come to Earth in spacecraft, I have *never* been abducted by Them.

I have learned from my encounters that we have been kept in the dark about a lot of things. It seems that the media are obsessed with rehashing the negative stories of aliens, because there is so much trauma associated with them. The media love to exploit trauma. It's about time that someone be allowed to talk about their spiritual, nontraumatic, experiences with omniscient human Beings that come to Earth in spacecraft. This uncensored book will fill that bill and allow you to learn that there are positive encounters going on right here on Earth that have nothing to do with the Greys or reptilian aliens.

My encounters started around 1976—well, at least that's what I thought at that time. At first, I felt skeptical about what was going on during these experiences. They tested my belief system, because I had never heard of people living on other planets, let alone visiting Earth. I wondered, if they were real, then why me? Where did I fit into the big picture?

I had lots of questions and doubted if these events were really happening. I was raised as a Christian and taught that anything that goes bump in the night or was of an unknown nature could possibly be the work of the Devil.

I didn't feel negative energy coming from these Beings, in fact, it was the total opposite. My experiences with Them felt positive and more real than my everyday life.

I had moved to Orlando, Florida around 1973 to be near my cousin Ann. Prior to moving to Florida, we both lived up north. When the encounters were just starting, I got a surprise visit in the middle of the day from Ann. She came to me at work and said she couldn't wait for me to get off for the day. She had something urgent to tell me. I took my lunch break to see what was so important. She said she had just gone to get a psychic reading and it was totally accurate.

I was shocked. I didn't know she believed in anything like that. Our family thought of psychics as frauds that did readings solely to get your money. She confessed that she had previously had readings with this man, and he had been right on the money then, too—no pun intended.

I was happy for her if that was what she wanted to do with her money, but I didn't care to get involved. She was jumping up and down with excitement and told me that I had to get a reading with this man right away. I expressed my disbelief and said that I didn't care to waste my money on him. She told me he only charged ten dollars and she continued to insist that I get a reading. I was still skeptical.

She had not planned to give me all of the details as to why I should go. She wanted me to be surprised. I wasn't budging, so she finally told me that my name had come up in the reading, and the psychic told her that my life was about to change in a huge way. He didn't reveal any details to her but explained that he had information I needed to know about.

Finally, I gave up the argument and agreed to go and have the reading. After all, it was only ten dollars.

She made the appointment for me and drove me to get the reading. I'm glad I gave in now, because he put me on a spiritual path that I had not planned on heading toward. The end results made me a happier person than I had previously been.

During my reading, he gave me a lot of information about my future. I was totally shocked. He knew about things in my life that I had never told anyone. These things were spiritual gifts that I had, visions of the future and that kind of thing. I didn't know they were spiritual gifts yet. I assumed they were normal and that everyone experienced the same thing.

Having visions and getting warnings seemed normal to me, but as it turned out, I learned that not everybody has premonitions on an ongoing basis the way I do. Of course, there are many people that have that gift, but Ann agreed then that it was not a common way of life, and not for her, either.

This man also told me that I should read some spiritual/metaphysical books to help me to understand my gifts.

He also told me that I would be teaching others what life was really all about from the spiritual point of view. He said I would be well-known in the future for the knowledge and new understanding I would bring to the people of the world.

He gave me the name and phone number of a lady named Bonnie who was a friend of his. He said that she had a metaphysical church. It was on the far side of town from where I lived at the time.

I proceeded to get the books that he mentioned and some others that I felt led to read as well. Reading through them soon became boring, though, as I knew exactly what the books were going to say. It seemed as though each one was about my spiritual gifts.

Even though I was bored with them, I did learn that my experiences, which were varied in the metaphysical sense, actually had titles. I learned that having visions is called *clairvoyance*, and that hearing verbal messages telepathically is called *clairaudience*. I also learned that *X-ray vision* is the ability to see through solid objects with the naked eye. I have experienced X-ray vision twice in my life since then, and I was glad that I had read about it in advance. Otherwise, I would have thought I was hallucinating during the experiences.

I called Bonnie's office, per the psychic's instructions, to inquire about her church and any classes that she might be teaching. I was told that she did give classes on meditation.

I took the class to learn how to meditate and pray properly, so that I could align myself with a higher consciousness, where all the truth about everything is. I was really impressed with Bonnie, because she had such a wonderful energy and believed in God. It was essential for me to align myself with someone that believed in God for this type of teaching.

I decided to go to her church in Orlando. I asked my friend Sue, who was also interested in learning more about this type of spirituality, to go with me. She agreed to but when we got there, we were not sure if we were brave enough to go in. We had never been to a metaphysical church before, and we didn't know anyone that went there, which didn't help. We sat in the parking lot watching people enter the church. They all looked perfectly normal, like everyday people, but we were still chicken.

You have to remember that we were the products of our past teachings, or should I say, past brainwashings? Even though the classes and the books felt right, we were looking for some sort of guarantee that we were not walking into some kind of weird situation.

We couldn't work up the nerve to go into the unknown, so we drove away. During the week, Sue and I talked about how Bonnie seemed like such a normal person. We decided that we were being silly with our fears, so we made plans to go back to the church and actually make it inside this time. The next Sunday evening, we arrived on time and walked bravely into the church with the rest of the crowd.

It was a wonderful, spiritual service. We were drawn to a group of people from one family, and they became our best friends. I now consider them to be like my own family. It was interesting to us that these people lived on the same side of town as we did. We had traveled quite a distance only to meet likeminded people that lived near us. We enjoyed the service and meditation so much that we started having regular, weekly meditation sessions with our newfound friends.

While attending this church, I also met an American Indian by the name of Joanie who played an important part in my life at that time. She was a friend of Bonnie's and they had been working on a plan to open a larger spiritual center. Joanie became a special friend to me and led me on a path that helped me add more pieces to my puzzling mission in life.

We felt stupid for being afraid of this church after meeting all of these wonderful people there. In reality, they seemed like people we had known forever. We felt we were in the right place at the right time and with the people we were supposed to be with. Our initial fear just showed us how strongly we were programmed to live someone else's truth, until reality stepped in to show us our own.

That Sunday night, as Sue and I were driving home from church, we had an amazing experience. Through this whole church situation, we were starting to be guided toward our lives' intended paths, paths that felt right for both of us.

We were traveling on I-4 in Orlando. When we got near the Princeton Road exit, something mesmerizing happened. We were chatting about our evening when all of a sudden, Sue pointed toward the black, night sky and yelled, "Look! Do you see that?"

She was freaked out. I looked up and saw a spherical or globe-shaped object descending from the heavens. It was a blue-green color. My first impression was that it looked just like a traffic light lens. I was thinking that there couldn't be a stoplight that high in the sky. The object looked a lot smaller than it actually was, as it was still quite a distance away.

It was traveling fast and then started to move slower as it got closer to us. I could tell then that it was huge compared to the size of a single traffic light lens.

The entire globe was one solid color, but that color kept changing. These colors were more vivid than any I had ever seen before on Earth, almost as if they were alive.

The first color, as I mentioned previously, was an unusual shade of blue-green, brilliant and glowing. Then the entire globe changed to yellow right before our eyes, then to blue, and then to red as it glided down toward I-4. When it got close to the treetops, the object changed to a dazzling white.

The craft travelled horizontally at a very slow speed as it crossed over I-4. It went right over the top of all the cars and nonchalantly glided along like this was a normal, everyday occurrence.

It came really close to the front of our car as it crossed over I-4. I thought it was going to land right on top of us from the angle it was heading on. I slowed down to avoid getting hit. It was eerily close, but for some reason, I wasn't afraid of it. I was mesmerized. Time stood still for me.

It seemed obvious that it was going to land, hover, or even go into a body of water nearby. There is a lake in that area, but we never knew for sure where the craft ended up. It went down below the treetops on the west side of the Princeton exit and out of our sight.

I was amazed that it came that close to us with so much traffic on the road at that time of night. If it was trying to get attention, it certainly got ours. It was a miracle that there were no auto accidents, since I am sure everybody else was watching it as well.

The strangest thing about it was that there was no audible sound coming from the object. It was close enough to us that we should have heard some kind of sound. It was certainly controlled by some mechanism as it glided slowly and effortlessly across the sky.

I was so curious that I wanted to drive to the area where it seemed to land. We wanted to investigate the unknown, but being the chickens that we were then, we dismissed that idea pretty quickly. If I had it to do over again, I would have tried to see where it ended up.

I drove straight home and called the sheriff's department to report what we had seen. We wanted someone to check it out. I gave them a brief description of the object but decided that I couldn't say we had seen an unidentified flying object (UFO). It was my first sighting of a UFO, and I felt quite sure that it would be their first sighting as well, if they saw it.

I was so flustered that I ended up giving them a report that seems ridiculous now. I told them that it might have been a meteor, and maybe it hit someone's house. I was sure that it was not a meteor, as it looked manufactured and perfectly shaped, but I wanted to know that someone in authority actually saw this UFO before I said that I had. We assumed that something like this would be investigated.

We checked the papers for a few days and didn't see anything about it. We hadn't considered that the police wouldn't report it to the news even they had seen the craft. After all, it was 1976; people were still very naive about UFOs, I know I certainly was. I had never heard anybody in my circle of friends mention UFOs.

I later heard that there was a prominent business owner in downtown Orlando that had reported seeing an alien craft in the area as well. His business was not very far from the location where the globe went down.

This sighting seemed to trigger a series of encounters for me with various species that arrive in spacecraft. Most of them were with the Enlightened Ones or Light Beings who I refer to as the Messengers from God or The Nine. The other species I mentioned did interact with me sporadically for a few years and then disappeared from my life. The Messengers are still with me, and my experiences with Them continue to be the most meaningful and purposeful of the encounters. They are and have been orchestrating and guiding me on my mission.

The Nine are a very diverse group. I would estimate that I had approximately twenty different, in-person meetings with these Beings over an extended number of months.

I was somehow transported to Their location for each visit with Them. This always happened in the afternoons. I never knew where I went or how I got there because I didn't ask. I eventually learned that I could ask questions and wished I had taken advantage of being there with Them to ask more. At that time, I felt as if these encounters were Their meetings, and I didn't want to take up Their valuable time asking questions. I just wanted to hear Their message and find out more about Their purpose for me.

In these meetings, They were always sitting on the same side of what appeared to be a long, narrow, conference table as They faced me. They all appeared to be about the same height when in a sitting position, yet They all looked different.

The main Being, who seemed to be in control of the meetings and me, has a sort of bronze-colored skin with jet black, straight, shoulder-length hair. He has beautiful jet black eyes, too, that glisten as if they have gold flecks in them. In earthly terms, I would describe Him as a Bronze God.

However, His skin isn't exactly bronze as we know it. It is so difficult to describe, because I had never seen that color of skin before. It is a combination of colors: bronze, copper, and red.

The bronze-skinned male always sat in the middle, and the others sat on either side of Him. As I've said, He was always in control of the meeting, and somehow, caused me not to look around the room. I don't know if I wasn't physically able to look around, or if I was just transfixed on His striking looks and message. Needless to say, I was mesmerized by what was happening and by His unusual appearance.

I could see some of the other Beings very clearly, in my peripheral vision. These were the ones that sat closest to Him. One of Them has long, white-blonde hair, and He faced me to my right. To the left of the Bronze Being, there was another male who has lighter brown hair. They all looked very human; They were approximately the same size and build, yet individual in appearance.

There were four Beings on either side of the central one, making a total of nine at each meeting. That number is one of the reasons I started calling Them *The Nine*. They prefer I call Them that or Messengers from God, as opposed to Their real names, so that we do not get caught up in Their names and miss the message.

They've always gotten right to the point without wasting any time. They are always very business-like but in a loving sense. I could tell that I was dealing with humans that are not from Earth because of These humans have an intense spiritual energy, omniscience and the power to lift you off your feet.

Almost every time I met with Them during that period, They showed me the same technical piece of equipment. They wanted me to have it produced on Earth. It was something to help with physical ailments. My problem was that the words They used to describe it to me were not words from our vocabulary. They were too technical as well.

They would tell me the names of the parts and how to assemble them while I was in Their presence. In those meetings, I understood exactly what They were showing me, because I was in a higher state of consciousness. Words really didn't mean anything—I simply knew what They meant instinctively. I knew the names of the parts in *Their* language, so to speak. I could not remember what the words meant when I was transported back into my home to get the job done.

All of the species seem to operate in a different mode of time than we do. Everything moves so fast for me when I am in Their presence. My human brain has a hard time grasping and remembering every little detail after returning to Earth. I don't lose all the information that I learn when I am with Them, thank God for that. What I usually lose track of are things that are very technical.

It is very cool to be in Their presence and in this high, spiritual vibration where I can know anything that I desire. I am able to think a question and know the answer to anything I want to know. It is like being in an all-knowing energy. I guess you could describe it as a universal language.

When our meetings have ended, I found myself abruptly coming back to Earth inside my home. The reason I say abruptly is because, when you are engulfed by Their loving and peaceful energy and then thrust back into earthly energies, it is almost like being shocked. Earthly energy is so negative that it is almost depressing compared to Their energy, anyway.

I would be very aggravated with myself then, when I discovered that I was back home and couldn't remember the technical details of the equipment. They went to great lengths to assemble it, take it apart, and reassemble it over and over again in my presence. Each time, They would ask me emphatically, "Do you think you can remember it this time?" Each time, I assured Them that I could. I completely comprehended it in those moments. Needless to say, They finally gave up on that venture and moved on to other things that They wanted me to assist Them with.

These next meetings were and have been about changes that were and are to come to our planet. These changes have been geographic in nature as well as societal changes. The Nine want me to be instrumental in helping people on Earth. During these Earth-change meetings, They have shown me movies on a screen that were really about what They wanted me to see of the future in general and the changes to come to Earth. The movies have been created and shown to me in a way that has made these changes appear to be happening in the moment.

That kind of visual effect was and is easier for me to remember. I was finally in familiar territory. The movies have been realistic to me, but I haven't been fond of the experience considering that I have had to be traumatized by these events twice. I have seen them on the screen and then again in person or on television as they have come to pass on Earth.

In reality, there is no such thing as time, as we know it. Everything past, present, and future are all happening at once. Basically, I've lived the changes on the screen in what felt like real time, according to the dimension I've been in when I've seen them. This would be considered the future in Earth time but it has felt like the present to me. When the changes have occurred on Earth, I have witnessed them again. This is where trauma has come in for me—in having had to experience these events twice.

All of these energy-charged meetings seemed to create a physical side effect for me at first, due to the amount of intense spiritual energy that The Nine possess. Their high frequency energy penetrated my aura or body. It would last for quite a while after the meetings and felt very unusual. I eventually got used to it.

All of the encounters I am aware of have occurred when I am in an alert, wide-awake state. If they have ever occurred when I am asleep, I don't know anything about it and honestly, I don't think I really want to know if that is the case.

I like to think that I have free will and so far, this has always been granted to me by Them. I have always been given the choice to accept or reject Their actions taken with me.

There are people on Earth that have been taken without their permission, as depicted in various television shows about alien encounters. During one of my own, I was told that people would not remember the encounters they had that were unpleasant, if they had not had a regression performed. They said that some of the procedures are kind of like having surgery. If you had a regression regarding a surgical procedure, you would also be traumatized since you would remember the details and pain.

Up to this point, I have never had a negative experience that I am aware of. Quite the contrary. The Beings that have been around me have had such a wonderful, loving energy. Their main focus is on pure, spiritual love. This is all that really matters in our world and Theirs. With it, everything can become perfect. Their message is for us to send love to all people and all things in order to create peace, harmony, and happiness in the world.

Chapter 2
Electrical Encounters of the Earthly Kind

Over the years, I have been totally amazed by how a lot of the bizarre events that have taken place in my life were seemingly orchestrated or controlled by some unseen force. If that's not the case, then I certainly have had a lot of miraculous coincidences.

When the following events took place, I was not aware of them being connected or controlled by anything. However, I was not able to explain them any other way.

Unusual events became more noticeable and frequent in my life after my meetings with The Nine had begun. During each, I somehow absorbed Their intense spiritual energy. The best way I can describe what I have felt and absorbed when in Their presence is that it is almost like an intense electric current but loving, peaceful, and balanced.

The energy They emit and I have absorbed has caused many interesting side effects. The result has been a number of electrifying experiences of the earthly kind.

During one of my encounters with The Nine, I was told telepathically that I would know when They were around because the lights would flicker, or there would be power outages. Both have occurred on several occasions.

These phenomena have been witnessed by several of my friends. Davey, a friend who traveled with me a lot, started noticing them and other fascinating things happening around me when they first began. He was amazed and fascinated by it, after he got over being spooked. He would call these strange events to my attention if I didn't seem to notice them. He would always say, "Whee-ooh! They're back."

Most of the times that The Nine have been around me on Earth, I have known They were there without seeing Them. There's no denying Their presence, because I can feel my skin become electrified and my hair follicles stand up.

All of this extra electricity within my cells either has created power outages or caused electrical items to blow out in my home. When it first started happening, I basically blew up everything that I touched; my dishwasher, heating and air-conditioning unit, toaster, hair dryers, and six audio cassette recorders all blew their circuits within a couple of weeks.

At first, I didn't put two and two together. I kept returning the recorders to the store, thinking they must be faulty. The store manager finally refused to replace the recorders after several returns. He told me that I must be causing the problem.

These encounters became more frequent, and the electrical events started occurring in other places besides my home. In public places, there would be frequent power outages as well.

I finally told a few close friends besides Davey about what was happening. Of course, they were curious and wanted to witness one of these electrical events. I couldn't make plans for them to witness one, of course, but two friends, Sue and Karen, got their chance when we went to dinner at the 94th Aero Squadron in Orlando. The building lost total power while we were looking at the menu. Thank God, this happened at a nice restaurant that had candles lit all over the place.

After a little while, the power came back on and the server came by to take our order. I just had to ask if their power went out on a regular basis. She said the manager was surprised by it, because an outage had never happened before that he knew of.

Another time, I was driving through the southeastern United States. All of a sudden, something told me to stop to get gas and a bite to eat. I stopped at a gas station to find that their power was going out. I drove to another one nearby and their power went out on me as well.

I decided I would eat first and then get gas at another location. I stopped at a restaurant, got out of my car, and walked to the door. The manager came out to greet me and said they had just lost power.

I was starting to think this power outage thing wasn't so much fun anymore. It could have been only a weird coincidence but if so, I certainly seemed to have more than my share of them.

Deepak Chopra says that there are no coincidences, only clues to your path in life. I understood that concept, but I didn't understand what path these coincidences were leading me on yet. The one thing I had learned was that when these events took place, I had avoided a disaster by my delay. I found that to be true on several occasions.

Not too long ago, I told my sister about some of the power outages that had happened, and she reminded me of a couple of times that I had completely forgotten about. These two occurred while I had been visiting her up north a few years back. We visited some of the old places we had lived at as children. Just as we arrived at one of the spots, the power went out.

By that point, I was so used to these electrical events that I had totally forgotten about those particular events. I had not been interested in telling my family about these electrical events then, anyhow. Only a few close friends were privy to them and my other experiences. It was too hard to hide the occurrences from those friends, because they were becoming involved in the encounters.

There was one particularly unusual event. I had gone to my attorney's office for a visit. When I entered the building, I learned that their power had gone out. I ask him what had happened to their electricity. He said that, the minute I drove into their parking lot, the power to the entire building went out. At first, I thought he was joking with me.

My attorney is a valued friend, so we took advantage of this down time to catch up on our lives. The power company arrived and spent two hours trying to locate the problem. They checked everything, both the fuses and wiring inside and out. They couldn't find the problem so they left.

At that point, I gave up and decided to leave. My attorney's secretary called me at home to tell me that the power came back on the very minute I drove out of their driveway.

I told Karen about what had happened at the attorney's office, as she had witnessed the power outage at the restaurant in Orlando. Now she was more curious than ever and wanted to turn it all into an experiment or test, so to speak. She challenged The Nine to prove these power outages were coming from Them. She asked Them to create another one that night.

We decided to go to a movie that evening. We stopped in the ladies' room inside the theater. The minute we went in the room and closed the door, the lights went off. It was pitch black. We opened the door to see if the hallway lights were on. All of them were.

We walked into the hallway and waited for a couple of minutes, then peeked back in the bathroom. It was still dark. We waited another minute or two and looked again. This time, the lights were on. Needless to say, Karen was a little more than spooked. She decided not to test Them again.

I'm not sure how this energy can always be around me and be so extensive and powerful. It seems to be with me no matter where I go. Just recently, I went to a mall in North Carolina. While I sat at the stoplight in front of the mall, the light quit working.

I proceeded to drive into the mall parking lot. It was about two in the afternoon by the time I found a parking place. It took about ten minutes to walk the distance to the mall door. A security guard greeted me. He was chatting with another guard, and they were getting ready to lock the doors. He looked at me and said, "You can't come in. We just lost power in the entire mall; we have to close it for now."

I recall another weird incident that didn't seem to be electrical as far as I could tell. I had gone to a meeting with my attorney friend at his other office in the CNA building in downtown Orlando. I parked in a high-rise, parking garage. On my return to the parking garage after the meeting, I walked past the automatic ticket machine. As I did, it started popping tickets out like crazy. They flew all over the floor.

A man in a uniform came running over to me. He acted like a policeman who had just seen someone commit a crime. He said he was the parking lot attendant, and he wanted to search my purse and briefcase. I allowed him to do the search, and of course, he found nothing unusual.

He was a little embarrassed at that point and said he was sorry to have searched my belongings, but that he had to account for each ticket. I guess they were numbered. He was really shocked at what had happened. He kept apologizing to me and remarked that it was not possible for the machine to just pop out tickets when someone walked by it. He said it was the first time that this had ever happened, and he would have to write up a report and have me sign it to account for the tickets, because nobody would believe him otherwise.

He wasn't sure what made the machine malfunction but alluded to the possibility that I might have had a large amount of metal on me or in the briefcase. I assumed he thought I had a gun; I wasn't really sure what was going on, but I gladly signed his report. I felt sorry for him and was afraid he might get in trouble over the missing tickets.

I felt like I was on *Candid Camera*. After the fact, I had to laugh about it. It struck me as being so funny to see those tickets flying out of there and shooting across the cement. I wondered if he were just pulling my leg for his own entertainment. The expressions on his face and his actions didn't seem like that were the case, so I went along with his orders.

I never had any proof that it had anything to do with me, but he certainly seemed sincere with his alarm about the whole situation. Needless to say, I never parked in that garage again.

I was later surprised when I was led to read an article in *OMNI* magazine that described other people with this same electrical outage problem. I believe they referred to them as *electric people*, and the article definitely confirmed for me that the phenomena were not imaginary since it turned out I am not the only one that has had similar incidents.

I often find a sense of humor in my bizarre adventures. All of my guides have a great sense of humor as well and sometimes entertain me with it. Don't get me wrong; They are not pranksters. They don't do that kind of thing. They are deeply spiritual and very serious and sincere about Their work on Earth. They just don't go about doing it in a doom-and-gloom manner. I feel very lucky to know "people in high places" like Them.

I guess you could say that They treat Their work matter-of-factly. They are working with the *isness* principle: dealing with reality and the way things actually are. They know that we need help to save the Earth and ourselves; that's just how it truly *is*.

There was one point in my conversations with Them when They became very serious. They brought up how I called Them *aliens* and corrected me on that. In a gentle way, They told me They didn't like being called that. They said, "We don't call you aliens, so why do you call us aliens? You are just as foreign to us as we are to you." They also said, "We are actually 'Brothers of Man' and prefer to be called by that title."

I know and respect Them as much or more than I do my immediate family members on Earth. I had only used the term *aliens* for earthlings to be able to understand what I am talking about. The general Earth population has not yet been educated on the fact that there are Brothers of Man living out there in the Universe. This book will bring that knowledge to the public so we can correct this issue of name calling. In the future, we will freely call them Brothers of Man and everyone will know Whom that refers to. They will make Themselves known, not only through me but also on Their own in many different ways.

This applies to the Beings that guide me. These particular Beings think universally, in a way that I have grown to more fully understand. They see us as equals, in a sense. We on Earth judge everything and try to put everybody in classes or levels. This is the big difference between earthlings and beings from other planets. A large number of people on Earth do not realize that we live in the same Universe with other life-forms. Most earthlings have a naïve point of view; they don't even recognize that there is life on other planets.

I am quite sure that all of this will change quite a bit in my lifetime. We will all be faced with an entirely new reality.

Chapter 3
Chance or Fate?

My life had started to take on a new meaning now that I realized that I had a purpose with the Brothers of Man, also known as The Nine. I was becoming more enlightened as to what was real and what wasn't. With this newfound knowledge, I decided that I better start following my guidance and instructions a little better.

At this point in our lives, Sue and I felt we were on the right path for our journey through life. I found it interesting that we were both led to these new studies at the same time, studies of natural law or spiritual law—God's law.

While I considered this change in my life, I flashed back to a time when my psychic friend, Joanie, told me that I should move forward with my spiritual studies. Unfortunately, I didn't follow up on that at the time. It had felt right in my gut, but I was so busy that starting to pursue it kept getting pushed back farther and farther.

Joanie was one of the most spiritually gifted people I had ever met who had not arrived in a spaceship from another planet. Her father was a Winnebago medicine man. She had given me an intuitive reading on several occasions. During each, I was told I had a great spiritual gift and that I should go to Cassadaga to study with a minister by the name of Joseph. She was very emphatic about this and stressed how important it was.

Approximately two years had passed before I finally drove to Cassadaga to find Reverend Joseph. Joanie had told me that he taught spiritual classes in his home, and she was very emphatic about this path for me. I had planned to make an inquiry with him at some point; however, I had let other things get in the way. Then one morning I awoke with the compelling sense that I had to go to Cassadaga. It was imperative that I find Reverend Joseph. I also knew if I didn't go right then I would never get it done. I have learned that it is absolutely necessary to act upon the guidance that I get when it comes with urgency.

I knew the Reverend's name but didn't know where he lived, so I decided to let my spiritual GPS guide me in the correct direction. When I got to the edge of town, that spiritual GPS kicked in, and I felt a pull and a knowingness that I should turn to the right just as I got to the street he lived on. I realized that I had made the correct turn when I saw a sign bearing his name on the lawn. The guidance had been impeccable; I traveled straight to his house without a hitch.

I got out of the car and knocked on the door. His wife greeted me. I asked if I could get information on the classes. She informed me that he no longer held them, as he was terminally ill and in bed most of the time.

My heart sank. I had waited too long to follow my instructions. I was mad at myself because I was supposed to have taken his classes to further my spiritual evolution, and now I had lost the chance. I was very upset that I had not made the time to come see him earlier.

I thanked her for the information and started to leave. As I turned to my car, she paused and then said, "Wait a minute, Joseph said he wants you to wait. I will be right back." She went inside for a few minutes then returned, "He wants you to come in and talk to him." She led me to a bedroom where he was lying down. Then she left us alone to talk.

Right away, he jumped enthusiastically into conversation. The first thing he said was "What took you so long?" I stared at him with a puzzled look and tried to figure what he was really asking me. I had never met him before, and there was no way he could have known anything about me. He also didn't know where I lived, so he wasn't asking about the length of my drive.

He proceeded, "I knew you were coming here; my Guides told me you were coming. I have been waiting so long for you. They have kept me alive for you to get here, and I wasn't sure if you were going to make it in time."

Needless to say, I was in utter shock.

He told me that he was presently speaking to my master spiritual Guide. He asked if I knew the name of this Guide and who my other Guides were. I told him that I didn't know who all of them were, but I was aware of the one he was speaking about. He said it was important that I know who all of Them were and to start listening and following Their guidance more often. He also said he wanted to restart the classes so I could attend. They would be held by his wife. She would teach them under his guidance, and he would sit in with the class as often as possible.

After I got back home, I immediately called Sue to tell her about my bizarre meeting with Reverend Joseph. We both decided to sign up for the classes. I have to give thanks to Joanie for her guidance on this matter.

The classes started right away. The Reverend was there every night. During each class, he gave me important messages for my future path from his Guides. They all came to pass just as he said. These classes felt as though they were being held specifically for me, even though there were other attendees.

After the series had ended, his wife called me. Joseph had been taken to the hospital for his final days, and he asked her to call and advise me of his condition. He also wanted me to know that he had been instructed to tell me the names of each spiritual Guide and Their purpose with me before he passed away. She wanted to know if I would give him permission to do that. Of course, I agreed.

A short time later, she called again to explain how important our meetings and his outlining the Guides for me had been to him. She repeated that several times and then added that she hoped I realized how important it was that we had finally met. She went on to say, "It was the last thing he did." He finished dictating the information to her and said, "My work here is done." Then he passed away.

She invited me to come to a memorial service for him since he and I had had such a strong spiritual connection. Several friends of mine from Bonnie's church also knew who he was and wanted to go with me to his memorial service. I asked them to ride with me. At that point, things took another unusual turn.

As we were driving to Cassadaga, I saw lights flashing up ahead. A highway patrol car had pulled someone over, but I couldn't see what was going on.

Right before we got to the flashing lights, my car started sputtering. I was concerned it was going to die on me, so I decided to go ahead and pull off to the side of the road. We coasted to a stop and ended up right behind the police car, just as the last drop of gas was used.

The officer walked over and asked me if there was a problem. I explained that my car must have run out of gas, and that we were driving to Cassadaga for a memorial service. I had neglected to check the gas gauge with all of the stress and excitement of getting ready to go. I was always cautious and checked my gas gauge every time I got in my car. This was the first time I could ever recall running out of gas.

The officer understood our time crunch and offered to take me to get some gas in his car. He was happy to take me to the next exit and was very chatty on the way. He asked me about Cassadaga, mediums, and psychics as we drove. He also asked me a lot of spiritual questions, as if I were an expert on the subject. I felt as though I was able to teach him something from the things that I had recently learned through Joseph and Bonnie's classes.

The officer said he had always been curious about spirituality. He wanted to get a psychic reading but was scared of the whole idea. I explained that my experiences had always been highly spiritual and beneficial. He was relieved to hear that and seemed to take my word for it. He ended the conversation by telling me that he would get a reading someday.

He asked me to take his phone number and keep in touch on the spiritual matters we had discussed. He seemed to be serious about his spiritual path and was amazed at the way our meeting had taken place. He felt it was an omen, and it meant something special to him.

I later had a dream that it was his birthday. I called to tell him about it. He told me it was true: it was his birthday. He decided to invite all his friends over that weekend for a cookout to celebrate.

He also said that he had a new outlook on mediums. He felt positively about them now, and again commented on what an unusual situation our meeting was. He thought our contact was a good omen for him, and that I had been very helpful for him and his spiritual outlook.

I later received a note from him. He wrote that after my call, he reflected again on how our meeting had some spiritual connection. He went fishing the next day, and every time he threw his line in, he caught another fish. He couldn't believe it. He was catching them by the dozens.

He told me about how he felt this unusual and amazingly large catch was another spiritual omen. With it in mind, he decided to celebrate his spiritual birthday along with his regular one. He held the big cookout as planned except that he served all the fish as a way to share his spiritual connection and adventure with his friends. I was quite surprised at how all of this turned out and how important our meeting truly was to him. It was good to know that such a small thing was so meaningful for this officer. He had an entirely new spiritual outlook on life and was very happy about it.

So many good things came from taking those classes. Another bonus was that I made a new friend from one of the class attendees, Terra. Terra and I have remained friends throughout the years, and I gained her entire family as an extended family by meeting her there. I later realized that Terra was not only a friend for life but she was also the administrator for the business owner who had reported the UFO sighting in the same area where Sue and I saw the spacecraft. A few years later, a very personal thing occurred in my life that I needed the assistance of law enforcement to deal with. I knew just whom to call! The officer I met on the way to Cassadaga came to my rescue once again.

Chapter 4
Visitors, Earth Changes, and Reincarnation

I was starting to see more of the big picture now that I had become aware of my otherworldly Visitors, The Nine. I was already getting a lot of guidance from my angelic spiritual Guides, the Ascended Masters, but now I had an added bonus. I realized that both They and The Nine would be guiding me along life's path.

I feel as though I am here on Earth for a specific purpose, a mission of sorts. I was curious about the full scope of that mission when I realized what powerful guidance I had with me. I had felt the unusual presence of these Visitors, but I didn't understand it.

With that curiosity, I allowed The Nine to guide me on a regular basis. They have an extremely intense energy that is very identifiable. It comes with a feeling that I can only describe as *pure* love and perfect balance. I was able to call upon Them at almost any time if I needed Their assistance. They even taught me how to meditate properly.

In this teaching, I was shown how to mentally relive an extremely happy time to change my vibrational frequency. It would change to a higher level, that of a love vibration. This allowed my energy to be more conducive to Theirs and made it easier to communicate with Them. This process was extremely helpful for making me more balanced.

After They had worked with me on this process for a while, I became more aware of how negative our earthly energy actually is compared to Their energy, anyway. By functioning in a love vibration, I realized that I was able to stay positive even with the negative energies all around me.

I am the person who is often called upon to be the motivator for people who need help in their life struggles. I can see now that I have been getting Their guidance all along. I feel that this is partially due to my desire to help others.

These Light Beings continue to pop in to communicate with me at any time and place, usually in the most unexpected places. Their communication is done by telepathy and visual communication processes.

They often give me dictations as I am writing. They have even transmitted lengthy poems to me that are so amazingly beautiful. Their words and poems flow like music.

They sometimes give me instructions in advance to meet with Them at a specific time and place. These meetings are normally quite an adventure because They don't usually tell me why I am to meet with Them. They are varied in intent, but the end result is always very purposeful and meaningful. These meetings have even been witnessed by others right here on Earth.

Most of the visits with the Light Beings occur during the daytime hours but always when I am in a wide-awake state, as opposed to a dream state. During each, I am given specific instructions. These instructions are varied and never the same. Sometimes, I am just guided as to what my next step is, and other times, I am given predictions for the future.

I received detailed information regarding Earth and societal changes that were and are to come. For a while, these were numerous and continued daily.

After a while, They instructed me to do research on safe places to live and preparedness tips for survival and a better way of life. I also had to locate maps of fault lines and bodies of water to prepare one that would show the safest places to live. I was even instructed to teach people how to grow food inside their home.

While compiling all of this information, I added a list of resources for dried foods, nonelectric items, and general information on the canning of food.

After all of this information was prepared, I was told to give lectures and classes to disseminate the information.

Then early one morning, I was awakened to the sound of a powerful voice that came to me telepathically. This particular morning, the Visitor was talking to me about Florida.

The room was filled with intense energy, and I could feel the presence of a Light Being there with me. I can always identify Them by Their vibrational frequency and know exactly where They are in the room. Normally, I do not see Them in solid form, but it is as if the Beings are solid at the time They are present. I feel and sense Their energy, even though I don't always visually see them. In one sense you could say that I see them with my mind's eye, or third eye.

Their energy is intense and electrifying. Each of Their vibrational frequencies is as recognizable to me as a human's face would be if I saw Them visually. The difference is that I just sense who They are rather than see Them. It is sort of like knowing Them from a sixth sense. I recognize them by Their individual frequency. The level of Their frequency also defines the level of spiritual evolution They have achieved. If the Light Beings were to appear to me in Their partial Light-bodies, then I would see figures that have a shape but are surrounded by a White Light aura. When coming to me on Earth, there is no reason for Them to use that much spiritual energy to identify Themselves because Their energy is Their identifier. It is very natural to know who They are without seeing physical bodies.

When I first met The Messengers, I immediately recognized Them on a soul to soul basis. I knew Them from my gut or knowingness. If an Enlightened Being came to me that was not one of the Messengers, I would feel it as well as sense it, and I would also recognize Them, assuming They had previously paid me a visit and introduced Themselves to me.

That morning, this familiar male, Light Being appeared to me and started giving me telepathic information, and suddenly, a movie with great clarity rolled right before my eyes. It was created for me out of thin air. I was watching Florida in the future.

As I watched, I could see that approximately two-thirds of the lower part of the state was underwater. Not even a blade of grass was sticking out. I was told that earth changes would occur that would put a portion of Florida totally underwater.

The film took place live in that time period, when everything was already underwater. It was after the disaster had occurred; I did not see the actual process take place. Years prior to that, I had seen a tidal wave hitting land in a vision, but unfortunately, I didn't see the location of it, so I don't know if that is what the cause will be.

However, I do know beyond a shadow of a doubt that Florida will, at some point, end up looking the same as I saw it. I find it hard to comprehend, but unfortunately, I know it is a truth. I just wish that I had been given an idea of when this would occur.

As you might imagine, I was totally shocked and saddened at seeing and hearing about this. I was so depressed and tired, all I wanted to do was to go back to sleep and forget about what I had seen.

I was told to get up and draw a map with the details of what I had been shown so I wouldn't forget any part of it. I assured Him that I wouldn't forget and proceeded to go back to sleep. Each time I attempted to fall asleep, I was abruptly awakened and shown the whole thing again. The entire vision and message was repeated three times. I finally got up and honored the request.

I drew a map of the state of Florida to indicate where the land would be left intact. I drew a fairly straight line that went from Leesburg to the west coast. On the east coast, my line started around Ormond Beach and angled downward to meet the line at Leesburg. I feel that line is really close to where it should be. I had to estimate approximately where it will be, as I was not given any names of cities at that time.

This encounter prompted me to eventually relocate to an area above where I saw the new water line. I was still living in Orlando at the time, and according to the film, it would be underwater at some point.

I had seen many other earth changes in my visions of the future, especially along the eastern coast of the United States. I was even taken out of my body by a guide and underneath the central part of Florida where I observed these vast areas of void or open spaces. There wasn't much holding the earth above me, except for a few pillar-like formations that looked like what you see in a cave. These pillars appeared to be of a limestone quality.

On another occasion, I had a vision of a map that depicted a large pie-shaped chunk of land that had disappeared along the coast of North Carolina. That line started near the northeastern border of the state, went inward, and then back out and down.

Other areas of major earth changes that I saw were along the New Madrid fault. These were due to earthquakes in this particular area or fault line but I specifically saw an earthquake in Memphis. I also saw that New Orleans would be going underwater. This was prior to that actual event taking place. Then I saw what looked like the entire state of Maine fall right off the map and into the Atlantic Ocean. The other things that I saw were shocking, of course, but to see that large chunk of land fall all at one time was very disturbing.

At the time that I had the vision of Maine, I couldn't recall which state was located there, but when I looked at an actual map, there was no guesswork. My vision of this map was identical to the actual one.

I do not like being the bearer of bad news or doom and gloom, but this time I must follow my instructions.

In other visions, I saw that our atmosphere was in grave danger; the sunspots were bad and the ultraviolet rays were harming our eyes and skin. At the time when I was having this particular vision, I thought that the scientists were holding out on us. They weren't saying anything about these problems yet. Why wasn't anyone warning people? That's what my logical mind was asking when I'd see the future effects. I guess the experience of knowing in advance was part of the answer to that question. Maybe they hadn't realized the problems yet.

I proceeded to give lectures and classes after doing my research to gather all of the pertinent information. I discussed and shared the earth changes that I had seen. I also shared my research papers along with the map that I had created of the areas that were going to be affected. I did not give a time line for these events, as I had not been given that information.

Some time later, I got a phone call from Cathy, a woman that attended one of my lectures in Atlanta. She told me that she had seen a story in the Atlanta newspaper that spanned several pages. She said this article covered the same topics that I had talked about in my lecture.

In the story, the writers discussed our atmosphere and other problems that Earth was experiencing, as well as a lot of other information about earth changes. This information came from various scientists, as I recall.

Cathy sent me a copy of the newspaper article. I was quite shocked when I read it because so much of it was exactly as I had been shown.

Whenever Cathy saw a news story of an earth change that had occurred just as I predicted in the lecture, she would send me a copy of it for my documentation. I had quite a large collection in a short period of time.

I continued to follow instructions as I received predictions on earth change events that were to come. One day, while meditating, I was shown that I should go to the Spiral Circle Bookstore in Orlando to purchase a book called *Rolling Thunder*. I believe the author was Jochman.

By this point, I wanted to stop receiving these disturbing visions and messages because it was very stressful for me. I followed the instructions anyway, I had learned a long time ago that when my Visitors talked, I should listen. I immediately paid a visit to the Spiral Circle and found the book right away, just as described. As I scanned through it, I saw that there were several psychics from eons ago featured in this book. They had made predictions on earth changes as well. I didn't want to be influenced by their predictions, and I wasn't sure what I was supposed to get from this book. I put it on my bookshelf to await further instructions.

A week or so later, I received a clear message while in meditation. That message consisted of one word, "Hildegard." I instantly flashed back to seeing that name in *Rolling Thunder*, and I knew that this was the answer I had been waiting for.

I stopped my meditation and grabbed the book to see if I could find the name in it. There it was. Hildegard predicted earth changes and gave some timelines for them in this particular book. A lot of her predictions, in general, were the same as the ones that I had received and lectured on.

Hildegard also talked about Haley's Comet passing over, and said that this would be the beginning of a series of floods, fires, earthquakes, volcanoes, and famine. That, in a nutshell, is what I had seen for the Earth, except that my predictions were detailed and specific. She also described the United States as a melting pot of nationalities.

This information reminded me of a message I had received in the past. In it, I was told that a lot of people would have their past karma erased when Haley's Comet passed over.

I believe that we create our destiny with our own power of thought and emotion. So in a sense, people would be starting over when this happened, and their choices would be made with their own free will; they would create their destinies. It would be a turning point for people, a time when they could choose a path to try and make the world a better place. I have seen a shift in that direction by many since then.

I received information that the Earth's vibration would change to a higher frequency after the comet. When this happened, people would start becoming more "in the know." They would become more in harmony with all that truly is. They would have a stronger gut feeling about the changes that were to come in their lives, and stronger intuitive feelings that would guide them to make drastic changes, if and when it was appropriate for them.

By making these necessary changes in their lives, people would actually bring more peace, harmony, and safety into them. This, in turn, would also bring better health to each individual because of the harmonious situations they had chosen to put themselves in.

I was also told that some people would try to ignore these feelings of change because they were too much trouble. Those who resisted the feelings would have difficulty because they were not going with the flow of nature. This, in turn, would create dis-harmony and dis-ease.

The passing of Haley's Comet was also supposed to bring forth an energy that would allow people to better understand what God is all about. This energy would create an uplifting, spiritual feeling for each person, if they allowed it into their lives. It would help them to know what their purpose on Earth, in this lifetime, was all about.

Now that I think back to the time when Haley's Comet passed over, I can see that there has been quite a bit of spiritual awakening since then. Unfortunately, the earth changes have also escalated as predicted.

I have seen a lot of people adapting and changing with this new spiritual energy. I have had a major increase in the raising of my consciousness during this time of spiritual change as well.

Of course, I have also had an advantage in this process due to my visitors, my Guides, helping me along the way. I believe that I've had Their guidance so I can help others.

My angelic Guides and the Light Beings have become my good friends, protectors, and companions. I am very grateful for Them because They have made my mission easier.

During this period of my life, I had been getting a number of detailed messages every week regarding these changes. I was disturbed by seeing all of them and frustrated because I couldn't do anything about it all. After the lectures were done, I asked that I stop getting the earth change messages so frequently. My wish was granted.

After seeing these changes to come, I made many of my own in my life. I couldn't believe how much time and effort it took to make these changes, including moving to safer ground, and I am still not done with them. There were a number of people that attended my classes and lectures who also relocated to new areas pretty quickly. They also made other changes to their ways of life to improve the quality of them.

I was grateful for all the changes that people made because I felt that I had fulfilled another part of my mission. It was only a small step in my lifelong mission, however.

The drawback to all of this dissemination of information about the earth and societal changes was that I was continually bombarded with phone calls and letters. People would see things come to pass that I had told them about, and then they wanted to know more. I couldn't keep up with the demand and was still trying to make a living, as I did not profit from this endeavor.

I met Ruth from Clearwater, Florida, as a result of the earth change lectures. She was very psychic and researched earth changes and safe places to live. We compared some of our notes on the changes and found that most of them were the same.

She read a letter to me that she had received from a friend of hers that was also psychic. This letter told about a dream she had had about Florida. In the dream, she saw a newspaper headline from Kentucky. It read, "Much of Florida is Totally Underwater." She gave the date of the newspaper, but I cannot remember it. I believe that dates of predictions are not carved in stone. I have read that raising consciousness and sending positive energy to anything can defer events or change things for the better.

This meeting with Ruth was very interesting, in that it gave me more confirmation of my visions and emphasized my need to relocate. At that time, I had not taken any steps toward moving yet.

The movie that I had watched about Florida, and the dialogue in it, was very powerful and left no doubt about the future that I had been shown. I felt more comfortable after I had given the information about Florida and the earth changes to the public. Knowledge and forewarning are power. When and if the attendees got a subtle warning to relocate, they might not ignore it after having been given the knowledge that these changes could be coming to pass.

I felt a heavy burden after seeing these earth and societal changes. I finally got some relief from it through meditation. During one meditation, I had an unusual experience: I saw my brain as an audiocassette tape. The tape was completely rewound, and many negative things were erased, which gave me such a clear feeling. I felt like the trauma of seeing the earth changes had been lifted. At that point, I became more relaxed and knew that I was on the right spiritual path.

It wasn't long before my instructions started coming to me in a different manner. I woke up one morning and began my usual meditation for daily instructions. I could feel a lot of energy in the room that caused me to be unusually wide-awake. Quickly, a lady appeared beside me and looked me right in the face. I saw her in the same manner as I see the Light Beings.

I thought I was in the twilight zone for a minute. She started to speak telepathically and said, "Well, you're——

aren't you?" She was calling me by a name that wasn't mine, a name that I recognized from history class.

I couldn't deny her powerful, female presence as she stood there by my bed, no matter what name she called me. She continued to speak loud and clear with a very strong British accent, and she went on to tell me that she had known me from a past life. In this particular past life, I had been a well-known historical male figure who had played a major part in the history of the United States. Needless to say, I was shocked about the facts she gave me, but they also made a lot of sense because I had felt a connection with that time in history.

She was surprised that I didn't recognize her, and that I didn't know about my past life as this male figure. She quickly created a movie-like vision for me. I watched myself make history in this past life while the movie rolled right before my eyes.

She also informed me about one of my missions on Earth that was yet to come in this lifetime. This particular mission was to be connected with that past life. In my mind, I assumed that it was why she had appeared there in my home.

With all of this information at hand, I became very curious as to who she was, so I asked what her name was. Just then, a solid ink pen and a lined tablet of white paper magically appeared right out of thin air. I was mesmerized by all of this, but I was still listening and watching intently.

Her answer was revealed to me as she used the pen to write her name across the lined tablet that she had just created. As it floated across the paper, she wrote the word

Bridges in fancy script. Her handwriting was beautiful. It was very ornate and artistic.

I felt as though she identified herself by her first name, as we seemed to be close friends from that lifetime. I will bet that her name went down in the history books too, but I don't recall anything about the name. She seemed to be a very well-to-do figure back in her day. She was prim and proper, and quite regal. She had an aura that felt as though she were financially well-off in that incarnation.

As usual, I was being my skeptical self during the encounter. I was thinking that this couldn't really be happening. She seemed to read my thoughts, the same way that all of these entities do who have the power to manifest. You can imagine the kind of thoughts you might have at a time like this. She proceeded to say, "If you don't believe the information that I have presented to you, then you should go to the library and research it."

She created another clear, movie-like vision for me that left no guesswork as to where I would find the information at the library. In the movie, she showed me the library number of the book that I was to read. She pointed out the exact location of the aisle that would have this specific book number on the end of it.

I had never been to my local library, so I drew a map with the location of the aisle and the number she had given me to speed things up when I got there.

Well, by now you know me well enough to know that I headed straight to the library that same day to get my proof. I'm always wanting my proof.

As I got to the area where the book should be, it fell off the shelf and into my hands. Sure enough, I found the numbers matched my notes exactly. These numbers and the book were located exactly where she said they would be. Oddly enough, this was the second time that a library book had fallen off the shelf and into my hands at a time when I needed the information in the book.

I learned that her story matched up with the story in the book as I read through it. This intrigued me enough that I traveled to the location of this past event that she had told me about.

After visiting the historical site, I was quite surprised by the feeling of connection I had to this past life. It became very real to me. During the visit, I saw that some vandalism had taken place there. I didn't pay much attention to it at the time but later that day, I had a flashback to the damage, and I was very emotional and sad about it. As this emotion ran through my body, it felt like I was transported back in time and that the feelings were coming from him and not me.

I know there is a mission to come from this historical awareness, but it is still a mystery as to how it will play out. I have also not yet found out whom she was in the scheme of things, other than what she told me that day. I think it will all become apparent when this upcoming mission is revealed to me.

I guess the problem with having these bizarre meetings and manifestations is that we have been so programmed to think that anything that goes bump in the night must be evil. Endless years, these encounters have been going on for me. So far, nothing negative has ever come from them, quite the contrary. The only time I get in trouble is if I don't listen and don't follow the guidance.

I was exhausted from seeing and experiencing so many past lives as I had begun to do. Seeing the earth and societal changes had also exhausted me. I decided that I wanted to accomplish all of my earthly missions and raise my spiritual consciousness in this lifetime, with the help of my Guides and the Light Beings. I learned through various metaphysical studies that if I accomplished all I had come to Earth for, I would move on to a higher spiritual plane of existence in my next life.

I also realized that one of the major reasons we are on Earth is to raise our spiritual consciousness. With all these realizations at hand, I changed my focus from a socially conscious life to one of a more spiritual path of existence.

During these spiritual encounters, it seems as though I have one foot on Earth and one foot somewhere else outside this earthly dimension. Each event surprises me because they rarely ever occur in the same manner. I never know what to expect. Just when I think that I won't have another encounter, up pops another one. Don't get me wrong; I am very grateful for the experiences. All of this has helped me to raise my consciousness and become who I am today, as well as given me the ability to help others.

I truly had to believe in reincarnation by this point. There were too many coincidences occurring in my life that pointed to reincarnation being a truth. I had met so many other people that believed in it as well.

One of these believers was a man that was very interested in Saint Augustine, Florida. He talked about it a lot. He said that he felt connected to that area, as if he had been there in a past life. I had never been there, but his enthusiasm got me interested. I called my cousin, Ann, to see if she would like to go there for a visit. She was very interested, so we set up a weekend trip that led to a lot of weekend trips to that area. I met several people there that I felt as though I had known in the past. When I mentioned it to a few of them, they commented that they also felt like they had known me forever.

One afternoon, I decided to meditate on Saint Augustine to see why I felt so drawn to that city. I really didn't get a specific answer, but I saw a large public building with distinct markings on the front.

This building kept haunting my thoughts, so I decided to go back to Saint Augustine to see if it existed there. As I drove into town, the building caught my eye. It was exactly like in my vision. It was a public building, and the front door was wide open, so I parked the car and went inside.

As I walked in, I felt very strange. There was dead silence and not a soul to be seen. The place seemed kind of eerie. I felt like I was somewhere I shouldn't be.

I quickly went into autopilot mode, even though I wasn't trying to. It was like something was guiding me without me having to think about the next move to make. Before I knew it, I had walked up a flight of stairs and was looking at several doors that had no signs on them. I found myself knocking on one of the unmarked doors.

Just then, I heard a voice say, "Come in," much to my surprise. I opened the door to find this pleasant lady, Anita, sitting at a desk. She invited me to come in and have a seat.

She started a friendly, personal chat as if she knew me. We then talked a couple of minutes about history, but quickly resumed our conversation about her personal life.

She was very concerned about her daughter who had been missing for a while. I was interested in what she had to say, so she told me the details. No sooner had she finished with them when something strange happened. I guess I was still on autopilot because my mouth opened and words came out, words that my mind had not initiated. Those words were, "Your daughter is in Colorado." I was shocked by what I was saying. She asked why I thought she was in Colorado. I simply explained to her that I was somewhat intuitive.

About that time, the door to her office opened, and in walked a male co-worker who needed access to files. Anita casually introduced me to this gentleman named Jerry, as he was leaving the room.

I excused myself shortly after the introduction as it was almost time for her to go home. As I was leaving her office, we exchanged our contact information. I asked her to let me know what she found out about her daughter.

I didn't hear from her, but I ran into her in a restaurant some time later. I approached her to inquire about her daughter. She said, "Didn't you get my letter? She was in Colorado. I heard from her while she was there. I wrote you because I was so amazed that you knew where she was."

Shortly after that meeting with Anita, I unexpectedly ran into Jerry when I was in downtown Saint Augustine. I didn't recognize him at all, but he approached me to discuss a meeting that we had both previously attended, although I did not know that he was at this particular meeting. I did not even recall what he looked like from our brief meeting at Anita's office, although he remembered me from both meetings. We talked for a while, and then he asked me if I remembered him. We had established that I had met him in the office building by then, but he kept asking if I remembered where I had known him prior to that.

I immediately had a gut feeling that I had known him in a past life, but I wasn't about to tell him that. I continued to name the places that I had lived to see if I had known him from any of them. He rejected all of the locations that I mentioned.

Upon parting, I asked if he would tell me where we had known each other from. His reply was, "You will tell me where you know me from the next time you see me."

A couple of months after that meeting with Jerry, I got a surprise phone call from Anita. She called to say that Jerry wanted to take me to lunch. I was puzzled but accepted the invitation, as she was a friend of his.

I decided to meditate before I went to meet him. I was still very curious to see if I really had known him in a past life. I was surprised at the results. I saw that I had been with him in a past life in another country. While I was in that incarnation, I had known that I would see him again in the future, and that I would recognize him by a ring that he would be wearing. It had a ruby stone in it.

I arrived at our lunch meeting to see what he wanted to discuss. I was taken by surprise when he asked me if I had recalled where we knew each other from. I really didn't want to tell him what I had learned about our past, so I avoided his question. He finally volunteered that he recognized me from a past life. He said that he instantly recognized me that day in Anita's office, just from seeing the back of my head. He went on to tell me more of the things that he remembered about our past life together.

After his confession, I was brave enough to tell him that I had meditated about us to see where I had known him from in the past. I told him what I had recalled about our life in another country, and that I also knew then that I would meet him in the future, and that I would recognize him by a ring he was wearing, a ring with a ruby stone in it. He raised his hand to show me the exact ring that I had just told him about. It was a ring that he wore almost every day.

I feel that Jerry will be involved with something in my future and he will be instrumental in that particular situation.

I have met several other people from past lives under very similar circumstances. It seems that we need to come back into new lives with people that we have known before, in order to work out unresolved issues from the past.

I have recalled a past life through a vision; it was with my current family. In this present lifetime, there are three children in our family. In the past life, we were the same three people as children, and we had the same parents. We lived in a house that is now a protected historic property in Saint Augustine. I had the opportunity to go inside this house. Its interior and furnishings looked like they did in my vision of our past, except for a piece of furniture that is now downstairs. It specifically caught my eye in the vision as I had seen us using it upstairs.

In this same vision, I saw what appeared to be the end of our lives in that house. All three of us children were lying on the stairs inside the house. I could see that we were lifeless. We looked as though we were draped there on the stairs. I did not see my parents at that time. However, I had seen them at this house at an earlier time.

After that vision, I had one more meeting with Jerry that I felt needed to take place. I had lunch with him again to tell him what I had recalled about this past life that involved current family members. I knew the general area where I had lived then but couldn't figure out exactly which house it was. He filled in some of the blanks for me about that location.

As I was reliving that particular past life, I saw that our house was in a waterfront area, but it was quite a distance from the water. I saw no other houses nearby. Saint Augustine is covered wall-to-wall with historic houses. I was quite sure that I knew which house it was except that there were others too close by and in front of it. At that time, what I had seen didn't make sense to me due to the other houses nearby.

Jerry gave me details about the house, which confirmed that my first thought was right. I still couldn't grasp the simplest part of the mystery, however. I relied on my vision of it and how I saw it back in that day. I finally realized that additional houses were built beside and in front of it after I lived there. So, at the time of my past life, there were no other houses nearby. I just had not taken the time for the logic of this issue to sink in.

In that same town, I saw another of my lifetimes and witnessed a female member of my immediate family there as well. She had the exact same vision of this as I did, and we both had the vision on the same day.

I saw myself as a man, standing and leaning against the old schoolhouse. I was fairly small in build and dressed like I would have been back in that day. I looked up and saw her walking toward the fort holding a stick that had buckets of water on each end. She was wearing high-top shoes and a long, red dress that had a small design on it.

The vision ended just as I saw a team of horses pulling a wagon and heading straight toward her. She was looking down and didn't see them coming.

When we discussed our identical visions, she realized that she could not remember what had happened to her that day. She knew she had a job but didn't remember what it was. I told her that she was a water carrier. She looked shocked and said, "Yes, that was it." To this very day, she is afraid of horses.

Things got more bizarre one day, when we pulled out some old pictures to share with family members. When we were in Saint Augustine, we had gone to one of those photography shops and had our pictures taken in old-fashioned clothes. We were both quite amazed when we pulled out this picture and saw the dress that she had chosen to wear. It was the same color and design as the fabric of the dress she was wearing the day she had walked toward the fort. Oddly enough, she still likes that same kind of fabric pattern and has owned a dress in this lifetime with that same design on it.

In another vision, I saw a past life in a different state. This vision occurred a few years after getting a message that I should look in the newspaper to find a property for sale. I got the paper and was then telepathically told which ad to call.

I did, in fact, purchase the property that was advertised. It was located near an abandoned gold mine. After purchasing it, I had a vision of myself in a past life. I was walking down the road toward the property. I was arm in arm with a man and wearing a long dress that looked very expensive. The man was also well dressed. We didn't look like we belonged in that area from the way we were dressed. I knew for sure that I had owned that same property in the past.

A few years later, an old newspaper article was presented to me that told the story of these gold prospectors who lived up north but had come down to this particular area to mine gold. I knew that I had been one of these gold-prospecting financial backers.

I found it interesting that I would be guided to buy that property for anything other than an investment. But as it turned out, it was more meaningful than I thought. More details may be shown to me in the future about it, but at least, it fits right in with my numerous so-called coincidences.

A few years back, I was scheduled to babysit for a friend's daughter who was under the age of two. The mother called me that day, before the little girl was to be brought over to my house. She told me that the child had been very ill the night before but was now well. The child had told her a fascinating and bizarre story about how she was healed.

The little girl told her mother that these tall men that she called doctors came in the middle of the night and took her out of her bed. The biggest point of the story was that she was excited that these men didn't know how to put her back in bed correctly. She slept in a youth bed with a rail that slid down.

She demonstrated to her mother how these doctors put her back in bed. They put her in it with the rail down and her legs hanging over the edge of it and left her that way.

I think her mother thought she might have been abducted by the Grey aliens because she had asked her daughter what color skin they had. She said that they had brown skin. The mother then wondered if the girl really knew her colors. She thought the child was mixed up, and that they were actually Greys.

That morning, when they went down to breakfast, she showed the child a brown lid from a jar. She asked her what color the lid was, and the child replied brown.

Before she came over to my house, I had set up a tape recorder because I also thought that she had possibly been abducted by aliens of some sort. When she got to my house, I let her play for a little while, then I turned on the tape recorder and started to speak to her about what her mother had told me.

She was really sharp because she corrected me whenever I said something wrong about what had happened to her. The conversation went something like this. I said, "Your mom said that these brown doctors came in your bedroom to heal you last night." She instantly corrected me by saying, "No, I said that."

At that point, she went on and on about an experience with these same men in her past. She said, "These mean men came in our house a long time ago, when you were my mommy and I lived with you. They came upstairs to me in that house. It was before I came to live with this mommy."

I asked if it was the same house that she lives in now, which I did just to see if she were imagining all of it because she also lived in a two-story house currently. She replied, "No."

She elaborated about her past experience with these men and said, "They were bad guys when I lived with you in that other house. That is why they had to come this time to make me well."

I then asked why she thought that they were bad then. She said, "They keeeled me with these long sticks that had something sharp on the end of them, and they hit me on top of the head." She continued, "The blood was running down my face a lot." She indicated that she was upstairs alone at that time.

This precious little girl was able to speak fairly well in sentences at that time, other than being a little dutchy on some words. I kept asking her what she was saying when she used the word *keeeled*. I wanted her to tell me instead of putting words in her mouth or making suggestions. She just kept repeating *keeeled*, so I finally asked if she was saying *killed*. She replied yes and then repeated it by saying, "Yes, they keeeled me."

I am positive that she was my child in a past life, and I had felt that even before this event happened. Fortunately, I am still able to spend time with her now; we are still close friends.

This story reminds me of my own childhood. When I was about ten years old, I was in an auto accident with my Aunt Norma and other family members. Right before the accident, I had a vision of exactly what was going to happen. I saw that we were going to be hit in the rear of the car, then knocked off the road and into a ditch.

We were driving on icy roads at the time, and I had been hanging on the back of the driver's seat while my aunt was driving. I think I was making her nervous because I was so nervous about the road conditions. I had also been chatting her ear off.

The minute I had this vision, I told her about it and asked her to pull off the road and stop so that we would not have a wreck. She told me to be quiet and sit down. I immediately dropped to the floor with my feelings hurt.

About that time, a car came flying up behind us as if he was in a long skid. He hit us in the rear and knocked us off of the road, exactly as I had seen it.

My aunt and two other family members were injured; my grandfather had nerve damage that he never really recovered from. The other children in the backseat were asleep and were not injured. I recall having bit my tongue really hard. My mouth must have still been moving; things haven't changed much in my life.

I remember that I didn't want to tell anyone about my visions when I was a child after that. I guess I thought they were a bad thing because I had been reprimanded by Aunt Norma. Biting my tongue might have been an omen to keep my mouth shut about these things, but now, here I go again with this book.

Years later as an adult, I went to visit Aunt Norma. Just as she opened the door to greet me, I had a flashback to the vision about the auto accident. I was shocked that I remembered this incident because I had not thought of it since the day it happened.

During our visit, I learned that she had been going to a spiritualist church and believed in these kinds of things.

I thought it was a good time to tell her about the incident that I recalled. After I repeated the story to her, I asked her if she had remembered that. Her mouth dropped open, and she said, "I do, now, but until you told me about it today, I had never thought of it over all of these years."

I could fill another book about bizarre coincidences and my past lives alone, or at least the lives that I have recalled up to this point. My life is a lot like a movie that I saw years and years ago. It was *The Reincarnation of Peter Proud*.

I watched this movie several times with a friend. We watched it over and over because we were mesmerized by the reincarnation aspect of it and how the pieces of the puzzle fell into place in his life.

Finally, one evening when the movie was over, we looked at each other and made the same observation. She said, "This movie is just like your life." She had taken the words right out of my mouth.

When I had watched that movie, I had only experienced a few of these strange coincidences, and it was right after the unusual events in Saint Augustine. I had just begun to realize that we have each lived many lives on Earth prior to this one.

After recently reviewing this movie to see if I was still impressed with it, I was surprised to find that it was not nearly as amazing as my life has been so far. That movie was almost boring compared to my life. The coincidences in it pale in comparison. Since watching it, my life has taken more intriguing turns than just learning I had lived other lives.

I have been grateful for seeing and reliving a number of my past lives, because it has given me more faith that we don't lie in graves for eons until Jesus comes back to retrieve us from them. Faith is something we all need, especially in this day and age. As you know, faith is one of the main reasons for this book.

In the early part of my guidance from the Messengers, I was told to write this book. They even gave me the title for it. I asked why I should write it, as I am not a writer. Their reply was, "Your life story along with Our messages will bring faith back to humanity."

After receiving these instructions, I was concerned, because I wasn't sure if I could actually write a book. I soon learned that They were going to take care of the writing of it.

They dictated information to me for the book, which allowed me to create it in the style They wanted it written. As it progressed, I found Them looking over my shoulder more and more to assist in the writing. They also continued to dictate new information that They wanted included.

They started the process by saying, "You will now write 'I now know beyond a shadow of a doubt that there really is life on other planets.' Make this the first sentence of the first chapter of this book."

During frequent visits, They saw me struggle with how to start chapter after chapter. Since They are omniscient, They immediately knew what I had written at the end of a previous chapter and what the contents of the next chapter would be, and so They dictated what They wanted the first few paragraphs of that chapter to say. After a few dictations in that manner, I had an Aha! moment; I completely understood the style of writing that They wanted done. They made what seemed like brain surgery to me look so simple.

So, for all of Their assistance and all I have learned up to this point, I am also grateful.

Chapter 5
Ask and You Shall Receive

Even though I had gained a lot more information about the things going on in my life, there were still pieces of the puzzle that had not yet fallen into place. I wanted to have all of the pieces at once.

I'm the type of person who is high energy, overly curious, and wants to know everything and know it now! At this point, I wanted and needed more details about my mission so that I could move forward quickly. I was feeling as though I had been stuck for a while.

One day, my life had felt like it were fairly normal, and then the next day, I started to realize that things were not that normal after all. In fact, from the outside looking in, my life was very bizarre, but still not as bizarre as it was about to become. Why were all of these unusual things happening to me? I guess all I had to do was mentally ask that question to get the answers.

After learning about the earth and societal changes that were to come and then seeing them start to escalate, I realized that major changes had also started occurring to my body as well. I now know that the changes to my body are due to the presence of the Light Beings that visit me; I just didn't know why they had happened then. I could see my life becoming one of service to humanity and to the evolution of Planet Earth, however. This made me realize that I needed to take better care of myself to fulfill these missions.

I feel that the Light Beings have constant contact with me. They seem to know what is going on with me and where I am at all times. I am not sure how They keep track of me. I have noticed that every time I am in the slightest bit of danger, or if anything comes up that They would feel a need to guard against, They are instantly beside me and assisting me in various ways.

I had always been a Christian, but with all of the unusual things going on, I felt a need to pray more and ask that I be able to speed up my missions and complete the tasks I was assigned.

The Bible says, "Ask and you shall receive." This held true for me as I prayed one night about all of my concerns. I got a quicker than expected response to my request. After I fell asleep, I was awakened from a deep sleep. I was so startled that I became wide-awake instantly, and the adrenaline was flowing.

I could feel a slight electrical energy in the air that filled the room. I didn't know what was going on. It was pitch dark in my bedroom and outside. It was so dark that when I opened my eyes, the black of night in my bedroom looked purple instead.

I have always been easy to wake up; it's like my body and mind are always sitting on "go." The slightest thing brings me to an alert state immediately; especially now, since so many unusual things have gone on around me.

Here I was, staring into the purple darkness, and I couldn't see a thing. Suddenly, a flexible object that felt like a small sandbag weight appeared out of nowhere and was instantly lying across my legs, between my knees and ankles. My first logical thought was that my daughter had come into my room and pitched my heavyweight robe across my legs to tell me that it was time to get up. That is exactly what it felt like, and it was what she usually did when it was time to get up.

I was expecting to hear her voice, but there was no voice, so I knew something unusual was happening. Things escalated before I could wonder why she would wake me in the middle of the night. It all happened in a flash.

I wasn't prepared for what happened next. I became very frightened as I heard a vibrating sound at the foot of my bed. It was a whirring noise, like something spinning at a high speed. It was extremely intense.

An energy started to build in the room as this sound grew louder and louder. It got to the point that it felt like the whole room was full of raw electricity. I don't know what raw electricity actually feels like, but this is how I imagine it to be.

In my mind's eye, I saw a large, circular shape of sparkling energy spinning at the foot of my bed. It rather reminded me of the way a large circle of clouds forms when there is a tornado. I saw this energy in a similar manner to how I see the nonsolid entities who visit me.

This energy pattern was quite large. My bedroom was approximately twelve feet by eighteen feet, and the energy I was seeing was about the width of my waterbed and more concentrated at the foot of the bed.

There was so much electricity in the room that you could light a bulb from the energy of it. I could still hear the buzzing. My entire body started to buzz as if I were getting a minor electrocution. I was so scared; it was all happening so fast. There was no time for logic to set in or to think things through. I was totally caught by surprise.

When my body started buzzing, my first thought was to turn on the lamp beside the bed so I could see what was going on. As I reached for it, a voice that spoke telepathically said, "Don't touch that lamp; you will be electrocuted." Needless to say, I dismissed that idea immediately.

By then, the energy had really built up. I saw white sparks appear in the air as I watched the energy pattern continue to swirl in a circular motion. I could feel it getting more intense as the buzzing grew louder.

My next thought was to turn onto my side to make this thing go away. I was reacting like a little kid that hides their eyes so that you can't see them. Before I could finish that thought, the whirling pattern at the foot of the bed quickly changed shape. Now it looked exactly like a tornado with the narrow part of the funnel coming straight toward me. My hair stood on end. The entire funnel of whirling energy went directly into the area of my solar plexus.

The whole time, my body was buzzing and vibrating with this energy. It didn't hurt like you might expect; it was just a major vibrating and tingling sensation. I was a little stunned physically, so my brain couldn't function for a while.

When I first had the thought to turn over, I found that all I could move was my upper body. As I raised my arms and turned the upper half of my body toward the lamp,

I discovered that I couldn't move my legs because of that wide band that had been placed across them. I was basically strapped down. It was such a scary feeling knowing that I couldn't escape or turn on a light.

I could feel myself still in my body and physically feeling what was going on, but there was a slight sense that part of me was an observer of the event. I dismissed this idea because I was seeing it with my eyes and feeling it with my body.

Obviously, I was still very wide-awake after the process had completed. For a while after all the funnel-shaped energy had completely entered my body, my cells were still buzzing with electricity. After they calmed down, I lay there for a long time to be sure the process was over. I was apprehensive about what might happen next.

This event might be better explained by something I found out later. Another self or another part of my original soul, for lack of a better way to explain it at this point, was trying to merge with the soul that I am now. As it turns out, we all have parallel souls or more than one branch of our soul. That is why we have soul mates. This will all make sense later as you read on.

This experience made me more involved with all of the earth changes that I had been researching and meditating on. I felt it was a way for the Light Beings to give me a jump start and get me going again on my mission. I started having a number of daily experiences that were even more out of the norm after getting my jump start. I recall another event around that same time when I took on the feelings and emotions of a traumatic event, but I didn't know why I was feeling this way.

In the past, I had picked up the feelings of close friends or relatives that had been hurt in some way. I would always have a knowingness that something was wrong or that someone needed help. I didn't always know whom the person was who was having the problem. I would call a few people and eventually find out whom.

A similar incident occurred this time but in a much more intense way. This particular evening, I had gone to bed early to meditate. I suddenly became terribly depressed and was experiencing all kinds of feelings of trauma. I kept saying to myself that I knew I was not feeling this way because of my own personal body, nothing was happening to me, but I still couldn't stop this horrible feeling. I prayed that it would go away, and it finally stopped before I went to sleep.

In a couple of days, I got a phone call from Davey. He told me that Beaver, a member of Davey's band and mutual friend of ours, had been in a terrible auto accident. He was paralyzed and asking to see me. I immediately told Davey that I knew exactly when it happened; it was Wednesday night, right? He confirmed that I was right and wondered how I knew about it. I told him about the experience I had gone through with the major feelings of depression and trauma that night.

Shortly after the phone call from Davey, I went to visit Beaver in the hospital. I told him about the experience I had the night of his accident. I told him that the feeling had been so real, but I knew it wasn't my trauma I was experiencing.

He then told me that he had wished he could jump out the window of the hospital. He explained that he didn't want to live in his current condition and truly would have jumped if he had been able to. He was way too active of a person and had a life that he wouldn't be able to live the way he used to. This confirmed that I had been picking up his feelings.

Over the long recovery, Beaver was able to regain his old, positive spirit and create a life for himself in music once again. He also desired to help others that were in the same position as him. He credits his emotional recovery to all of his close friends and support from his fans. They all kept the positive, loving energy going in his direction and sent healing energy to him as well.

For the most part, I feel like I am now a lot more able to protect myself from picking up other people's trauma. I receive a lot of feelings about things that are going to occur in the future, but now I know where they are coming from and why I am having the feelings.

Davey had been my friend for years, and we often took business trips together. No matter whether we were at home or traveling, something unusual always happened that amazed him.

All of these events had started to overwhelm me at that point in my life. With alien encounters, spiritual entities visiting me, and being shown the earth and societal changes for the future, I was definitely on overload. The logical mind does not always accept the unknown that easily either. Even though I had been going through my usual daily routines, my curiosity was always right up there in the front of my mind. I guess I wanted someone to give me a guarantee that what was happening in my life was real and not a figment of my imagination.

One part of me knew for sure that it was real, and the other part was saying, I have no proof of it. I kept thinking that these sorts of things just didn't happen in real life. I was constantly putting those thoughts out into the ether, hoping to get answers. I wanted proof that my imagination wasn't running away with me.

While these events were happening, they were definitely very real to me, but when I went out and about with my friends, it didn't seem like they were even possible. I will bet there are a number of people who have these same types of experiences and feel the same way, until they get used to them anyway. I have argued with myself many times over this.

Putting those curious thoughts out into the ether paid off when I met a woman through an unusual set of circumstances. She gave me more faith to trust in what was happening in my life. I was able to let down my barriers, somewhat. I realized that some of my mental and emotional blocks were due to the fact that we on Earth do not think universally. With this mind-set, it's difficult to comprehend that life can exist anywhere other than here.

After meeting her, I gained a better understanding about the possibilities that exist and then allowed myself to be more open. More and more encounters occurred after letting down some of my barriers.

This meeting came about after a series of twists and turns. It started one morning with my meditation. I was instructed to go to Cassadaga to get a psychic reading again. I didn't know all of the details but knew that if I were supposed to do this, I would be led. So with this faith, I headed to Cassadaga right away. I was so excited to see the outcome of the reading and hoped it would clear up some parts of my mysterious life.

As it turned out, I was led to the psychic that I was supposed to see. During the reading, I was told that I would meet a man with the initials B. A., and he would guide me to a woman by the name of Phyllis Schmidt, who was an alien abductee. I was told that she was well informed about aliens and UFOs. I tucked that information away and went home to wait for my next guidance.

A short time later, I had a feeling that I should go to the Spiral Circle again. As I entered the store, I saw a bulletin board that grabbed my attention. My eyes went right to the business card of the man whom I was to meet with. The name on the card had the same initials, B. A., as the person whom the psychic had told me I would meet.

I decided that the name on the card must be the man, so I gave him a call right away. I told him I didn't know why I was calling, but I knew that I needed to talk to him. He said he understood and that whatever came up in the conversation would bring about the reason for the call. During the conversation, Phyllis's name came up. I was surprised, even though I should have been expecting it.

I told him about my reading with the psychic and that he was to lead me to Phyllis. At that point, he told me that he knew her personally.

He said that she didn't live in Orlando, but he knew she would be in town in a couple of weeks. He promised that when she got into town, he would put me in touch with her. I didn't feel that I should wait that long, but I felt I had no other option.

As I hung up the phone, I felt an urgency about this meeting with Phyllis. I had a feeling that I should call Beverly, the owner of the Spiral Circle, where I found the business card. I asked her if she knew Phyllis, and it turned out that she also knew her.

After I explained to her that I needed to meet with Phyllis, she immediately told me that Phyllis was already in town visiting her daughter. She couldn't give me a phone number for her, but she offered to call and ask her to call me.

Phyllis called me quickly, much to my surprise. I explained why I wanted to talk to her, and that I had heard that she was a well informed on alien encounters. I told her that I was having what I believed to be alien encounters. I explained that I had a lot of notes from my encounters and asked if she would meet with me to read my notes.

I wanted to see if I was really having these encounters. Her immediate reaction was, "Oh, everybody thinks they are having alien encounters. Some are authentic and some are not." She was very hesitant about meeting with me and gave me the impression that she couldn't be bothered to waste her time on another kook.

She did, however, agree to meet and invited me to her daughter's home. As she opened the door and saw my papers in hand, she acted as if she knew me. I thought she must have recognized me as the phone caller. Her quick response was a huge smile and a warm welcome, which was totally different from her manner during our phone conversation.

I wasn't expecting her to be congenial at all. During our meeting, she referenced something that made me think she recognized me from a previous meeting. I had no idea what she was talking about so I just passed off her comment.

She looked over my notes and told me that my experiences were authentic. She confirmed that my encounters were real and indicated again that she knew who I was in a roundabout way. I was still puzzled because I didn't remember her from anywhere.

I showed her one of my notes that told about an encounter when one of these Beings told me they had been to the moon. They said that when They went to the moon, They wore suits of astor.

I didn't have a clue what astor was. Phyllis pulled out a huge book that seemed to be a dictionary. She thumbed through it and came up with the meaning. She said that astor meant heat and cold resistant, which made sense.

I told Phyllis about the piece of advanced technology equipment that I had previously been instructed to build, and that I was unable to remember it long enough to do anything with it. She told me that this information was already known. Another person had already built the equipment, another abductee in fact. With all of this information from her, I finally decided that I must not be delusional after all.

After I left the meeting, I drove onto the ramp to I-4. I suddenly realized that the round, globe-shaped object that I had witnessed floating over the freeway had gone down right in the vicinity of her daughter's home.

I later spoke with Phyllis's daughter to mention that I had seen a spacecraft go down around her neighborhood. She said, "Oh yes, we see them going into the lake in our neighborhood all the time." She also told me that her mom had recognized me from a time when we had had an encounter together.

Thank heavens for meeting Phyllis and for Beverly's assistance. I gained an understanding that a lot of possibilities do exist. The two of us couldn't be experiencing the same type of events with Beings from other planets or dimensions, if they were not real. I was now more convinced that all of my experiences were positive, as her past experiences were all positive. There also seemed to be some connection between the Beings that we each had experienced.

Beverly said something very interesting to me when I inquired about Phyllis. She said that she always knew I "had been wired." That didn't mean anything to me at the time, but later on, I read a book that said if you have alien encounters, then there is a possibility that you are wired. I don't understand exactly what that means, but I think of it as possibly having an implant of some sort. I am not sure if I am wired, but the Light Beings do seem able to have contact with me any time They wish, and They definitely know where I am at all times.

Beverly had an intuitive sense about the exact book that I needed to read, even when I didn't ask for her assistance. Each book that she suggested filled in one more piece of the puzzle.

Now that I had met someone with similar experiences to mine, I realized that all of this was really possible; I always wanted proof that my experiences were real, and I now had a little more confirmation. I was thinking about how I needed proof for myself, because I was continually being instructed to be public with my life. With those thoughts rolling around in my head, I suddenly heard a loud and clear, telepathic voice say, "God has spoken; let it be known."

That statement took me by surprise, but I never know what to expect with the kind of life I have.

With all of this knowledge, I was ready for the next chapter in my life. This experience with Phyllis made me get more involved with the earth and societal changes that I had been researching and meditating on. At that point, I started receiving more and more information that I was to share with the public.

As I mentioned earlier, there had been another businessman who reported a spacecraft sighting in the same general area where I had the meeting with Phyllis. As I left the meeting with Phyllis, I again noticed how close his business was to this location. Then I had a flashback. I recalled that Terra, whom I had met in the spiritual classes with Reverend Joseph, had worked in management with this same businessman.

Chapter 6
Aborted

I gained a lot of experience that would be helpful for me in the future as I continued to follow the directions and guidance I was given on my path. I had been told several times by the Light Beings to get involved with various public speakers and New Age personnel so I would become involved with more New Age projects.

I had previously invited a well-known actor and New Age speaker to do her seminar in Orlando. She was currently doing seminars in other areas of the country and did decide to do one in our area. I was invited to assist in helping with it. I worked with her staff during the three-day weekend.

I enjoyed assisting with the seminar as well hearing her speak. It was a fabulous success for her. I learned more about the coordination of such an event, though that was not my intent for inviting her.

This event led to my next set of instructions from the Light Beings. I was told to manage Jim, a well-known, New Age channeler. In fact, I had been given this message on several different occasions. I argued against it for a long time since I didn't understand much about channeling. I didn't even know if this guy needed a manager.

Some time later, I was invited by a friend to attend one of Jim's public-speaking engagements. During his seminar, I got a loud and clear telepathic message, "This is the one that We have been speaking to you about, in regard to management; this is him! Please contact him regarding this matter."

Even with all of those instructions, I was still skeptical about the outcome of contacting him. I went into meditation on it, and this time, a different Guide appeared to me. This time I saw his facial features very clearly. He was right in front of me and looked me straight in the eyes. He repeated the same instructions that I had been given about managing Jim.

I was quite shocked by this, especially since I was looking at the face of Saint Germain. I had no idea that He was one of my Guides prior to this visit. I had never seen His face in past meditations, but He seemed very familiar to me. Later on, I learned a lot more about Saint Germain's past lives, when He had incarnated on Earth. In one of those incarnations, He was a prominent historical figure. I felt connected to Him and that I had also been connected to Him in that particular past life.

With this latest visit from Saint Germain, I decided it was time to take a leap of faith and follow my guidance. I telephoned Jim right away. I spoke with him about the messages that I had been receiving about managing him. He had already been alerted about it prior to my call and knew that I was going to call him. As it turned out, the Entity that channeled through him wanted me to become his manager and Jim agreed.

I learned a lot from the experience of managing Jim. It was such a pleasure to be in close, regular contact with the wonderful, balanced, high-energy Entity that he channeled. I learned so much from Her. She made frequent visits to me on a personal level when Jim wasn't even channeling or in the area.

I also had several opportunities to have private sessions with Her through Jim. On one of those visits, I commented to Her that when the channeling was going on, I didn't see Jim at all. I was seeing the Entity even though I was actually looking at Jim. A jovial reply came back to me, "That's why you're the manager."

Being able to talk with this enlightened Entity was like becoming more enlightened myself as well as visiting with an old, true friend at the same time. She was someone that I had known forever.

The Entity also talked to us about earth changes that were coming. We were given specific details regarding preparations for upcoming changes. I was actually being prepared for my future of lecturing to the public about self-sufficiency for the times to come, although I wasn't aware of that fact at the time. "These were different from the lectures I had done previously about earth changes after the Nine first visited me."

I noticed that my bizarre encounters became more frequent while spending time with Jim and his channeling work. At one point, I was told that I was going to be taken by means of a spacecraft. I immediately said that I did not want to be taken in that manner. I had been hearing so much about abductions that were terrifying. The response to my objection was, "You will be taken; there will be no pain, and the pain you have now will be gone."

That message felt comforting, but I still wasn't too sure about it. In the past, when the Light Beings had given me instructions that I disagreed with, They allowed me the personal choice not to follow those instructions. I was allowed my free will, in other words. Of course, not following Their instructions was never the best decision. Many times, I later found that things would have turned out better had I followed those instructions.

I had a private meeting with the Entity that Jim channeled shortly after receiving the message that I would be taken by a spacecraft. During that channeling session, I was handed a tiny pillow. It was filled with an unknown substance. I was told to keep it with me at all times, day and night. Then I was to return it to Jim at a specific time. I felt it contained a spiritual energy, so I followed those instructions and was soon amazed.

I was home alone one evening and had the television on in the living room. I was working on paperwork in my bedroom that also served as my office. I suddenly felt a lot of intense spiritual energy in the room. Then I heard a voice speaking to me telepathically, "Lie down on your bed." I was puzzled by this request but was trying to comply with requests in general so I could fulfill my purposes and missions here on Earth.

I immediately lay down on the bed, television blaring and lights on. The minute I hit the bed, I felt an intense vibrational frequency in my solar plexus area. Before I knew it, half of my body's cells had broken apart and departed through my solar plexus. I could feel the cells as they proceeded to move out of my body.

I still had my mental faculties in working order, but I could feel myself floating in midair. I was floating toward the window in my bedroom. I knew immediately that I was going to go right through the window and outside. Needless to say, I was freaked out.

I started screaming because I didn't know for sure what was happening. I didn't realize at the time that it wouldn't hurt me to go through the glass. I don't understand much about how it would have worked, but I guess it has something to do with the vibrational frequency changes that take place. I now understand that I would have been able to pass through the glass with no effort and no pain. Since then, I have heard about this actually happening to many people.

After I screamed, this process reversed itself just before I reached the window. My cells funneled right back into my solar plexus area with a jolt. I was so freaked by this that I jumped up from my bed. I went to the living room to find the same television show on at about the same part of the show as when I had lain down on the bed. It was all so quick; very few minutes had passed.

Well, that was a perfectly good attempt foiled. I had just aborted an attempt to take me on board a spacecraft. Many times I have been mad at myself for being such a baby and often wondered what I missed by foiling it.

After this strange encounter, I had another visit with the channeled Entity to return the pillow She had given me. I neglected to ask Her what had happened to me that evening. I later thought it was strange that I didn't think to ask Her that. It was as if I weren't supposed to ask.

I was not very good at asking questions to the higher powers. I felt as if the purpose of Their visits was to give me information, and that it was a waste of Their time for me to ask frivolous questions. I had faith, and I discerned whom the Entities were by the type of energy each one emitted, so a name was not really required, and that's why I didn't ask for them.

My friends often asked me why I didn't ask other questions when these visits occurred. I finally learned that I could ask questions, and I was surprised to find that I actually got answers. It is hard to remember to ask questions when They appear to me. It is such a mesmerizing experience that questions are the last thing on my mind as I'm too busy learning from Them.

I also recall Them telling me that we on Earth get too caught up in throwing names of Enlightened Beings around. We miss a lot of the points to the messages because we are so wrapped up in the identities instead of the content. They obviously know best, and I can see that They have a very good point here.

A few months later, Jim and I were scheduled to do a seminar out of town. While driving to the hotel that day, I had time to think about my work and my missions here on Earth. I kept thinking about how my work managing Jim had started to take a new direction, a direction that I was not happy about.

As I thought it over, I became very upset. I felt that I needed to move on, but I wasn't sure if it was the right time to make the change. My gut was telling me that it was, so I put my thoughts out to my Guides and asked for clarity and direction.

After I got to the hotel that day, I spent time in meditation. I prayed to Jesus and asked for clarity about my working situation. I started centering myself and getting into my higher consciousness, when suddenly, I felt a very powerful presence in the room. My hair follicles were standing on end from this energy.

I quickly realized that the energy I felt was an undeniably male presence in the room with me. Since I had prayed to Jesus, I assumed it was Him. This male Entity started to communicate with me. I immediately interrupted His speech and asked, "Are you Jesus?" He replied, "No, I am Sunat Kumara. In the Bible, I am referred to as 'Ancient of Days.' I have come to tell you to leave your work with Jim and proceed with your own spiritual service. You have much work to do to help the people of your planet."

He talked about other things besides my work. He talked extensively about the details of Einstein's theory of relativity and that He was in agreement with Einstein. From the way the conversation was going, I felt as though Sunat were explaining how it's possible for aliens to visit Earth in their spacecraft. This is something for me to ponder after I get a better understanding of the theory.

It is unfortunate that I don't fully understand what the theory of relativity is all about. I do know what it is in general, but somehow, my brain failed to grasp the full meaning when I was in school. I would have been able to retain more of the exact details of the lengthy information that He gave me, if I had understood the theory to begin with. Although, I do feel as though I got His drift.

With all of that said, anyone that truly understands Einstein's theory would be able to put the pieces of this puzzle together. They may be able to understand that spacecraft travel to Earth from other areas of the Universe is possible.

I remained curious about Sunat Kumara and wanted to know more about Him. As it turned out, I had a book with me on that trip that contained information about Him. I had not read it yet, but I did after our seminar.

That wonderful visit with Sunat answered my questions about my work. A few days after, I met with Jim to explain that I would be leaving him to move forward with my own spiritual work. I was shocked to hear his reply. He said, "Yes I know; I was told by the Entity [the One that he channels] that you had your own public work to do, and that a Light Being from another planet was being sent to Earth to work directly with you and protect you at all times."

I continued to work with Jim for a while and then parted ways to work on my own mission. I remained in touch with the Entity that Jim channeled and attended some of his seminars as well as private sessions. She also paid visits to me in Her spirit body, also known as a soul body, when Jim was not around.

I later recalled that Saint Germain was the Visitor who had originally assigned me to work with Jim. At that point, I realized that I had fulfilled the mission that Saint Germain had assigned me. I was very grateful that Sunat Kumara stepped forward. He is the one who caused me to move forward on my life's path with His new guidance. I felt as though moving on was right for me after Sunat's visit. I might still be procrastinating about going public with my work if He had not paid that visit to me.

With the guidance of these last two Visitors, I had realized how wonderful it is that there are so many concerned Light Beings out there working with us for the well-being of our planet, as well as for all of humanity. These same Guides are very involved in assisting us with the earth and societal changes that we are in the midst of now and are still coming.

It became obvious to me that there was and is a much bigger plan for me after learning all of my new guidance. I knew beyond a shadow of a doubt that my mission was a mission of great importance. I felt very connected on a higher consciousness level to all of my Guides at this point in my life.

I was surprised when I read about Sunat in the book I had with me at the hotel. I learned that Sunat and Saint Germain had worked together on other missions in the past.

That same book also had a story about a time when Sunat asked God if He would be allowed to try to change people's way of life on Earth. He wanted to save them from their own demise. God agreed that Sunat could try to change them, but if it didn't work out, then God would proceed with His own plan.

This was when I realized how involved and concerned Sunat had always been about the people on Earth. I got more serious with my work and agreed to honor His wishes to get on with it.

Later on, I thought about my meeting with Sunat at the hotel and decided to look in my Bible to find anything that I could about Him, as "Ancient of Days," and there it was. I don't recall exactly where, but I do remember that it was in the early portion of the Bible.

When I first started receiving information about earth changes, it seemed impossible that things could actually escalate to the point that I had been shown. However, I saw these changes come to pass at a faster rate as time moved along.

I had done a lot of research after being shown the earth and societal changes by The Nine. After talking with Sunat, I regrouped and got back into preparing for the lectures and classes.

I had to gather numerous notebooks and audiotapes that I had created at the time these predictions were given to me. I kept a lot of tapes and notes after all the visits to have something to refer to. It took a lot of time and effort to put the information in a proper format. When I started writing the book, I soon learned just how much time it was going to take. It seemed never ending. It took years of part-time work just to compile the information before I could actually start the book. I have never taken a writing class, so I definitely had a huge obstacle to contend with.

As far as writing the book, it would have been easier to create a fictional account of encounters with beings from other planets. I wanted my story to be very specific in details, facts, and totally honest. I wanted it written exactly as I had lived it. I am a stickler for details, which caused me a lot more work, but it will be well worth it in the end.

Just as Sunat requested, my work of publicizing information I had been given was now also in its beginning phases. There was not much time for writing a book at that time due to the public work that I was embarking on of giving more lectures. I felt like I needed to be two people to accomplish all I had planned to do.

I met a lady named Paula while managing Jim. She was interested in working with me on the project of disseminating information to the public. She had previously done public speaking and editing as well, so she became my manager.

Per my previous guidance, the plan was to move to North Carolina to do some work on the public-speaking project and to continue to write this book. I think I jumped the gun on the timing of all this, due to my anxious state. I felt overwhelmed with all the work and that I was getting nowhere fast.

I was very grateful that Paula came onboard to help with this huge task. Her focus was to assist with the lectures and do part of the early-stage editing for a synopsis. She was the perfect person for this job, as she was a New Ager and had knowledge of the verbiage that would be used to describe the variety of encounters and Visitors that I had experienced. This was necessary to maintain the true story. By using these descriptive titles, the reader would be able to discern whom the Visitors were and which role Each was playing in my life.

When that work with the first synopsis was finished, she resumed her own work as a multi-talented speaker and editor. I felt like I was finally on my way to getting something accomplished, knowing that I had her assistance. Unfortunately, I am the kind of person that wants everything finished, and I cannot rest until it's done. Paula's help was great, but it barely made a dent in what needed to be accomplished. The end result was my being overwhelmed and working constantly.

I eventually had to temporarily discontinue a lot of the public work. Not only did I not have enough help, but my attendees started seeing the earth and societal changes comes to pass, just as I told them. This created so many requests for new information; I couldn't keep up with it. At that point, I had done a few lectures around the country, but I had to cut back on public work to finish the book and take care of life in general.

Chapter 7
It's Space Mountain Time

I had come to a point in my life when my choices were not my own. I was being forced into a situation that I wasn't emotionally or financially prepared for. There was one choice that I had made on my own during this incarnation: I wanted to become more spiritually evolved. I soon learned that my wish had been granted, and that I, indeed, had been chosen.

As it turned out, I was being forced onto the right spiritual and life path and didn't know or understand what was happening. I was sharing a house in Orlando with Sue. She announced a spur-of-the-moment decision to get married shortly. Now that she was leaving, I needed to rearrange my finances and entire life again and do it quickly.

I say again because I had just made a major, life-altering shift to enable this new lifestyle of spiritual work and study. I had already scaled down my expenses and did so again when I worked for Jim, the channeler. That was practically a volunteer position with spiritual benefits. Working with him was a part of my new path through life. After all, I had been instructed by my Guides to work with him. I was trying to follow through and conform to the instructions They gave me.

I also started getting frequent requests to volunteer for various community services. As a result, I spent a good part of my time in volunteer work. I also helped several other people financially, so this lesser income was a major adjustment for me.

I felt as though this new lifestyle was coming too fast for me. Most of my adult life had been lived in the fast lane. It felt as if I were on a treadmill with wheels. I had a good income, but that changed when I felt the need to slow down and shift my life to a more balanced and peaceful way of being. I felt a calling in my soul to that mission. Don't get me wrong; I still lived an overly active life. I had not become a monk yet.

I viewed the spiritual work and studies as spiritual growth and learning experiences. Money never entered my mind when I was involved with this new way of life. I was drawn to all kinds of positive and uplifting spiritual studies. They created a way of life that was somewhat removed from the socially conscious scene, but more importantly, it was away from the materialistic life that I had before the encounters began.

I realized when Sue decided to marry, that I was stuck between a rock and a hard place. I didn't see any possible way on such short notice that I would be able to afford a place to live without sharing expenses. It felt like the worst time I had experienced in my life. After thinking it over, I came up with a plan that I wasn't sure was the right thing to do, but it was the only option I had.

I knew that I had to settle somewhere because I had made a commitment to write my book and follow my spiritual guidance. I had to shut my eyes and do what I had to do. If I didn't, I could see myself ending up with no place to live. When I make a commitment to anything or anyone, I do my best to follow through, even to a fault.

Paula, the friend I had made through my work with Jim and who later assisted me when I lectured, wanted to move to North Carolina right away. She asked me if I would share rent with her there so she could start living in the area she had been drawn to relocate to. I had planned to move to North Carolina at some point but didn't feel ready to make the move just yet. I agreed to move with her despite it not being what I wanted to do. I wasn't really ready to leave Orlando. There were wedding plans to be made for Sue. I wanted to help with the arrangements, but Paula had already made her decision to move immediately. I had no choice; she was in control now, so I shut my eyes and made the move.

My friends in Orlando could not believe what was happening in my life at that time. They knew that I was always financially secure and in control of my material needs and my life. I felt like I was in shock and was very sad because I had no choice in these situations. The possibility of missing the wedding plans and my remaining time with Sue was traumatic for me. At that point, I had to go into survival mode and do what I had to do.

I did get to return to Orlando prior to the wedding so I could be involved with the plans. When I got there, I found that most of them were completed. At least I was able to be there for the wedding. I would not have been able to go if not for Paula. My dear friend offered to lend me her car to make that trip. I was more than grateful because my car was not in shape for traveling at that time.

I didn't understand the timing of what was going on. I do know now that I learned several personal lessons from the experience that have helped me through the rest of my life, but those were hard lessons. I learned that I should take more control of my own desires and wishes, even if it is a little inconvenient for others. I have always put other people's wishes before mine because that is the way I was raised.

After the wedding, I was still in shock at my move, because I realized I wouldn't be able to live near my best friend any longer. I was stuck with living in a strange place where I only knew one person. I had to get busy right away and try to forget that I had just lost my best friend. I had to move forward with my life. As I look back at it, I wish that I could have delayed the timing on the move. As I said, though, I was no longer in control of my life, but I could still begrudge the timing of the move.

Fortunately, things started to happen on the spiritual scene rather quickly in my new location. I didn't know it at the time, but there was a very specific reason that I moved to this location in North Carolina with Paula. This upcoming event could still have taken place at a later time, I think, if I had not made the hasty decision to move so quickly. At the time I felt that I had no choice if I wanted to have a roof over my head.

One day, while Paula was setting up her area of the new house, she decided to go out to get a few hardware items. She asked me to ride along with her to Lowe's to pick up her supplies. I was glad to get out of the house, so I went. I decided I would just sit in the car and enjoy some fresh air while she was in the store.

The minute she was out of sight, an unseen Visitor came with a familiar energy and a voice that was loud and clear—telepathically, of course. The Visitor said, "Thanks for coming to North Carolina; you will meet a man here who is going to help you." That was it, and then the Visitor vanished.

I didn't understand what that meant but I always listened and tried my best to follow instructions. Therefore, all I had to do was wait to find out what this new message was all about. Maybe They had me on a need-to-know basis only.

That evening after we got home, I recalled the time when I had experienced the aborted beaming process. During that incident, I could feel all of my cells come unglued and leave my physical body. I talked with Paula about this and told her that I didn't believe that such a thing was possible, even though I knew it had happened. There was no doubt or guesswork that this event had taken place. I somehow always managed to try to find an explanation that would prove that the incident never happened anyhow. So far, all I'd found was proof that it truly did happen.

Paula went into her bedroom and brought back a book titled *Unveiled Mysteries (Original)* by Godfrey Ray King. The Saint Germain Press had printed it. She said I should read the book and then I would understand it.

After two years, I was still working with that book; I couldn't get away from it. It was a great teacher for me and gave me an understanding of what was happening to me in some respects and of what was possible. It was just more proof that these things truly are amazing and possible.

Shortly after we were settled in our new home, Paula was away on a business trip. I sat at the desk, working on notes for a lecture that my Guides had instructed me to do in the North Carolina Mountains. I was totally engrossed in my thoughts when a Visitor, a Light Being, quickly dropped in to entertain me and then vanished again. This time, I telepathically heard the words, "It's space mountain time," in a humorous tone and manner.

It struck me as funny because I had just moved from Orlando where there actually was an attraction called Space Mountain. This time, it had a completely new meaning. I knew They were trying to comfort me, as well as let me know that They were on the job, so to speak, and that They were keeping track of me.

It didn't take long for me to find out what They meant by the phrase "It's space mountain time." They showed up frequently after making that statement. I would always feel Their overpowering energy, the energy that I was so familiar with and recognized as a Messengers' presence. Individually, each of Them would appear in the corner of my bedroom, especially on nights that Paula was out of town on business. Their energy felt like God, so to speak. It was extremely powerful and in tune with my soul. These visits often came after I had just prayed to Jesus, as I do each night. It was a very intense experience, however, enlightening.

As it turned out, this particular Visitor, one of the Messengers, had come to allow a transfer of intense spiritual energy, one of pure love to every cell of my body. I later learned that during the most intense energy transfers, another process was taking place. During these processes, I felt as though my body was being electrocuted, though this process never hurts.

While all of this was going on, a thought popped in my head that I had heard before. I recalled a time a few years back when I had been told that I had been chosen. When I asked why, the reply was, "Your prayers were heard when you said that you wanted to do what God had intended for you to do in this lifetime."

Then one night, while all of these intense energy visitations were going on, I heard another message telepathically. It was, "Thank God that you have been chosen. We will be back again in 88 days."

I was surprised to hear that They were coming back again in 88 days, at a specific time. I marked my calendar to check off the days. I wanted to see if They would return in precisely 88 days as promised.

I recall a night shortly after my second visit from Them in North Carolina. I was lying in bed and looking out the window of my second-story bedroom. I saw a huge white ball glowing there. It was a perfect spherical shape. It flashed off and on a few times as if to get my attention. I don't remember feeling sleepy or like I was going to fall asleep, but it was like I just disappeared. I also had a knowingness or a feeling that this white object had been perched there in the air for a period of time prior to my actually seeing it.

This bright, white, glowing object outside my window certainly wasn't the moon; it was a large vivid, solid object that was well lit. It was so bright that it should have hurt my eyes but it didn't. It flashed off and on like a spotlight but was too huge to be any kind of spotlight. At that time, I knew in my gut that it was definitely space mountain time.

On other occasions, I have experienced spiritual white light that was brilliant like this and didn't hurt my eyes either. It is the same principle as when you see people in heaven; there is always this brilliant white light glowing in the background, and it doesn't hurt your eyes. Colors in spirit form are more vivid than earthly colors. They seem to have light inside them that glows through them. It is the same type of color that I saw emanating from the globe-shaped spacecraft that I saw in Orlando.

The morning after I received this energy transfer, I awoke to an intense energy in the room. I could feel it penetrating my body. I saw so much that morning that I couldn't begin to tell you what it was; it was so complex. I looked into forever and saw things exactly as they are, not how we on Earth think about the way God and life actually is. I recall that some things didn't match up with what I had been taught regarding God and the Universe. I also knew that I would be shown more in the future, just not all at once the way it was happening this particular morning.

With all of this extra wisdom given to me, I felt I needed to look into some new spiritual studies and get involved with additional, like-minded friends in our new area. I stopped in the health food store to get more information about the area and felt drawn to a business card at the store's bulletin board or table; I'm not sure which it was. It belonged to a man named Van who lived in the area. He was a reflexologist. I was interested in reflexology for health reasons and found that it had been very helpful for me in the past.

I inquired with the store clerk about this man. I wanted a bit of a reference before setting an appointment with a stranger. She said, "He is wonderful. Everyone describes him as the man who fell from another planet." She added that he was very spiritually gifted in addition to doing a great health service.

Since I was certainly no stranger to Men from another planet, I decided that he would be a delight to meet. So, I checked him out. I called and set a time to consult with him about his service.

During our meeting, I learned that he had lived on the upper east coast of the United States and was well known for his amazing ability to heal. He told me about a person who was healed while in his presence. This particular person had come to him because they were paralyzed and unable to walk. He told me that the client levitated right off of the massage table while he worked with them. The client floated in midair and moved into an upright position and stood on the floor. The client was then able to walk. Van told me that he himself had been paralyzed at one point and healed himself through guidance that he was given telepathically.

Word got around about his work, and the miracle that had happened. He was bombarded by so many people that he finally had to move to the mountains to find peace in his life and continue his work.

After this visit, I was sold. I set up regular appointments with him. He indeed was very gifted and enlightened, as well as having a vibe that felt as though he truly could be from another planet, just as the store clerk had described him.

An intense spiritual energy surrounded Van that was projected to the client. I didn't know how powerful it actually was until one day after he had finished my treatment. When we were near the end of the session, his usual procedure was to use his hands to create an intense energy pattern that would continually swirl at the bottom of my feet until he stopped the energy. I had my eyes shut and was relaxing in a meditative state and didn't watch what he was doing. After the energy started, I always assumed that he was right there creating this energy pattern that I could feel swirling at my feet.

During this one treatment, I suddenly opened my eyes because I heard dishes rattling in the outer office. There was nobody in the office except the two of us, as far as I knew. I quickly opened my eyes to look at him and see what was going on. The energy still whirled at my feet, but he was gone. Finally, he came back in the room with me and stopped the energy from whirling. When he saw that my eyes were open, and that I was looking for him, he nonchalantly said, "I was just making myself a cup of coffee in the other office." He acted as if all of this were normal. Well, I guess it was normal for him.

During another visit, Van said, "I see a brilliant, spiritual, white light energy that is beside you now. It is the One of your parallel souls that is the original of you, the One who has maintained its divinity, the One who possesses full Christ Consciousness and has never chosen to incarnate in a physical body. This One is now ready to merge with you, *if you will permit it.*"

He went on to say, "You created or set all of these plans before incarnating eons ago; now, it is time. The other parallel souls are having too great of a time in what they're doing to be interested in merging. They could if they so desired, but that was not set out in the original plan."

Van also explained to me that he would battle with this or any Entity/soul that was around me, and he would do it immediately and permanently remove it from my existence if he did not know for sure that it was my full Christ Consciousness he were dealing with. He assured me that this One particular soul was, in fact, who he said it was.

In the beginning of this conversation, I noticed that he had said this Christ Consciousness wanted to merge consciousness with me *if I would permit it*. My knowingness told me that this was all true. So of course, I agreed to the merging as I discussed it with Van. This goes to show you that we have free will in this lifetime to make our choices.

For me, retaining less social consciousness and gaining more Christ Consciousness is the ultimate goal. Van explained to me that a merging of this type would take a long time, and the body would have to adjust to the process as it took place. The energy is so powerful that the body is not able to tolerate the intensity of this type of Christ Consciousness all at once.

Van was indeed a powerful man in his own rite. When he talked, people listened, since he was a man of many miracles and of powerful energy. Again, he was indeed like a man who fell from another planet. Thank God for Van.

After meeting him, I realized that he was definitely not like anyone else I have ever encountered here on Earth. I have met very enlightened people, but there is something different about this man. Strangely, I can't remember much about what he looked like physically because I always dealt with him more on a spiritual level and didn't pay much attention to his looks. Other than that, he had either very short hair, a shaved head, or was balding; I only vaguely recall his appearance.

Thank God my Guides led me to him. I had to give up many very personal things and socially conscious activities to make this move to North Carolina. Those sacrifices made me sad in the beginning. In the end, I was more than grateful, because of the soul enhancement that was starting and my health had greatly improved. I also learned so much about other things in my life from him.

While editing today, I was amazed to read this section about my divine parallel life. I had forgotten all about It–at least thinking about It in those terms. Everyday life is so full of time-consuming necessities that it is hard to find time to dwell on the things that we know and care the most about; I had filed the process I am going through with this divine life into the back of my mind. I realize now that the gradual merging has continued to take place, and it is almost too good to be true. It is sort of like winning the lottery.

As I edited this section today, a Visitor looked over my shoulder at the computer screen. Usually, this would mean I would receive a dictation, but there was none given. I felt as though He was just acknowledging my appreciation of how lucky I am to have these experiences.

I thanked God for allowing all this to occur for me in this lifetime, and for my ability to fulfill my life's mission even though I didn't then and don't yet fully know all that it entails.

We are now noticing the geographic changes and energy shifts on Earth. They are happening more frequently. This activity lets us know that there is a much more major shift yet to come. All of this reality is so hard to comprehend in human terms. With all of these events in mind, things were making more sense to me. Each step along the way had given me a better handle on what was and is going on in my life. I had major confidence in what transpired with Van.

I now realize that the merging had already started prior to meeting him, but I didn't understand what it was at the time that it started. I was grateful for the clarity that he gave me on that matter as well as the additional help he gave me. He had no way to know what had been going on with the energy transfers that had taken place in my life prior to meeting him, yet he seemed to know intuitively and was able to explain it to me and assist in the plan. He certainly filled in the missing pieces of the merging puzzle and other facets of my life.

I was now more accepting of the intense energies that had been imparted to me so often. Since then, I have often felt as though there are two of me—not a separate me, but I guess you could say that a part of me was noticeable that had not been in action before. It was now activated. I could see then that I had an extra sense, in a manner of speaking. A sense that has always protected me and responds to something before my mind knows it needs to respond. I always seem to be ahead of myself. Basically, I see it as using more of my higher consciousness and not just functioning with my brain.

In these instances, I do not feel another presence beside me or anything like that; it is more like an extra sense added to the normal five senses. I often read something on a sign and hear it in my head before my eyes actually see it. I will then see the sign with the exact words that I have just heard. On a few occasions, I have read something that wasn't there at all, only to find out that the same words were later placed on the sign. I saw it in advance of its placement.

This happened once when a pharmacy was about to relocate. I read it on the sign and mentioned it to the store manager. He asked me how I knew about the move. I told him I read it on the sign in front of the store right before I came in. He told me that it was not on the sign and took me outside to show me. He was right. It was not on the sign.

They were, in fact, moving, but he was not ready to tell the public about it yet. He was quite amazed by this and told me the new location but asked me to keep it confidential until they were ready to announce it.

There have also been numerous times when I have been saved from accidents or things of that nature due to this extra sense or additional presence. One time, I had stayed overnight at a girlfriend's house that was in a nearby city. I got up early the next morning to drive home without much sleep.

As I was driving, I realized that I had driven several miles down the wrong road. The road I found myself on took me about thirty minutes out of my way. I don't remember turning onto this road or driving the distance. I have no idea how it happened. It was as if I was not even present in my body, mind, or spirit. I basically had lost time.

When I realized that I was on the wrong road, I had a flashback to an early morning vision. I recalled the entire vision. I had totally forgotten about it the second after I had seen it; I was barely awake at the time.

As the entire vision flashed before my eyes once again exactly as I had seen it the first time, I saw the front page of the local newspaper. In the lower-right corner of the page, I saw my bright orange Firebird, and it was totally wrecked, smashed all the way around and on top. The newspaper story said I had missed the curve and rolled down the hill. There it was in full color: one big, crumpled, orange pile.

If my car had not taken the wrong road, I feel quite sure I would have had the accident. Some unseen force saved me. This was one more time that I thanked God for being chosen.

Another odd aspect of it was that the curve my car missed was within a minute or so of the place where I lived as a child. I have negotiated that curve many times without accident; it was very familiar to me.

I was happy to continue down the wrong road to get home. The extra thirty minutes became a nonissue; time was no longer of the essence at that point.

The unseen aspects of life are much more complex than any of us know or realize. I have been through so many different unknown and mysterious processes that were governed by the sometimes-unseen spiritual world. I don't doubt that there are many more mysteries that will be unveiled to me as well.

One of the mysterious things I have experienced is a process called *restructuring*. At least, that is what I have learned by going through this process a number of times. I don't have all the terminology down or a complete understanding of the technical things that transpire during the restructuring process, but it seems to be similar or is the same as the merging I have been experiencing. Van described that as the periodic merging of my physical body with my original soul, the spiritual consciousness that has maintained Its divinity.

However, I don't believe restructuring and merging are completely one and the same, however very similar, because the healing that I have experienced through restructuring seemed to come to me upon request or at times of serious conditions. I may see this differently as time goes on, or it may be explained to me by one of my Guides but for generalities they are in fact the same process, in a sense. Merging is an energy transfer of a divine soul. Healing is an energy transfer from a Divine Being. A soul merging is much more intense and powerful, however, in reality, both are energy transfers of a sort.

A healing of one type or another always took place at the times I experienced restructuring. This is because a physical ailment cannot exist after it has been exposed to the God Consciousness or higher spiritual planes of energy.

A little later in this book, I discuss restructuring in depth and outline a lot of the restructuring processes that have taken place for you to have a better understanding of that process.

Restructuring and merging of consciousness are both happening to me. They work together, which makes perfect sense to me now. As I learn more each day, it is more and more like a jigsaw puzzle with the pieces coming together to make a complete picture of what is happening with my body and my life.

Each time I have worked on this book, I get new information intuitively, or it is channeled through me to add to the subject I was writing about. I have to say, I have been quite shocked when I find the notes I have written about events like the mergings. In most cases, I had not recalled these events since the moment they happened until I read my notes. At that point, I vividly recall exactly what happened.

Possibly, my brain is still resisting the fact that these things are real, due to all of my past social consciousness programming. I have to admit, they don't fit in with what is known as a normal life on Earth.

While having my sessions with Van, I recognized the fact that a partial merging of the soul had taken place at the time when the Visitors had told me they would be back in 88 days.

Van told me that he had been taken by a UFO earlier in his life. He was taken to a planet made up of quartz crystals like the ones we dig from the earth on our planet. This prompted me to tell him about a very powerful event I had experienced some time back. It was more real than watching a movie. It was like I was taken into the future and witnessed an event yet to come. As I watched, I saw a spaceship landing in the Clearwater, Florida, area. I could feel myself there, and I was a part of what was going on. I saw exactly where the ship landed, and I have passed that location many times in my past travels.

A group of regal-looking females came out of this ship. They all looked exactly alike, as if cloned. They looked more like an Egyptian than anything else I can think of. Their eyes were slightly slanted like the Greys, but they were not huge; they were more human sized. They wore garments similar to what the women wear in India. These alien women were very striking and beautiful.

There were a lot of Earth people milling around the ship that looked like curiosity seekers. A large number of the cloned-looking Females mingled with them. I feel that it is important to point out that I feel that they were here to harvest humans but they were not forcing anyone to go with them. They were merely offering that opportunity to the people there.

These beings are not part of the Messengers and I didn't feel any personal connection to them. The energy that they emitted felt more like someone from Earth, as opposed to an alien Being with a powerful God-like energy. As far as I know, these Beings have not had any personal contact with me. I feel that I experienced this future event as though I was a part of it, merely for the purpose of knowing what will transpire in the future and be able to share this information with people on Earth.

Some of my family members were there during this experience of the future, and I was careful not to get separated from them in the big crowd of people. I was afraid I would be separated from them forever. At one point, I did get separated from one of them, and my Dad, who was already in spirit form at the time, came to me to assist in reuniting me with this family member. He was not there in physical form but in spiritual form only.

A part of me was scared, especially when I got separated from the family member; although, I was not afraid of the regal-looking entities. I guess it was just the fear of the unknown and the anxiety of possible separation.

After telling Van about this experience, he told me that he also had seen or knew something about these same regal-looking beings. He also told me that one of his

Guides had never reincarnated on Earth. This was very interesting to me because it made me wonder if my parallel soul that had never incarnated, had also guided me during my lifetime.

All in all, it was quite an experience working with Van. His energy was of a very high frequency. He seemed very close to God. He lived his life on a spiritual basis in every way. It was, indeed, as if he had come here from another planet. He was a very advanced soul.

I explained to Van how I had second guessed a lot of things when it came to powerful energies. There were times when I was a slight bit unsure about what was actually going on with all of this energy that had penetrated my body over the last few years.

He told me that I wouldn't feel this merging energy as intensely in the future in quite the same way as before. He said it was slowly being assimilated into my entire being. He explained that the energy of such a Being as was merging with me would be so intense that if It came close to me in full energy, and I put up a resistance to the merging, I would not be able to handle the intensity of It. God knows I am always resisting the unknown.

I can relate to this process more now because of the number of similar things that have happened to me since that first encounter with the merging process. I am sure there is more of this energy to come, and with Van's comforting method of explaining it, it has allowed me to welcome the merging.

When he explained all of this to me, my gut feeling was that he was right. I just needed someone to assure me that it was okay to allow this to happen, due to the unknown factor of it. It was just one more reason for me to have met Van and allowed him to work with my physical body. It was part of my desire and goal to achieve a higher consciousness in this lifetime, and for that, he was a great help.

When I told Van that my Visitors had told me they would be back in 88 days, he also marked his calendar to await the results. He placed a lot of significance on anything that had to do with the number 8. In fact, it meant so much to him that he got married on 8-8-88.

After Van talked to me about numbers and their significance, I recalled times when I had noticed various sets of numbers that reoccurred in my life. These were phone numbers and addresses that were always significant and meaningful. At those times, I could tell that I was going with the divine, purposeful flow. They were part of the right things for my path through life. I often used that method as a guide to tell me if I was at the right place or dealing with the right person. It gave me directions through life that turned out really well.

This type of thing with names and numbers seems to come in groups of three. Over the years, I have noticed that when a third person shows up with the same exact name as the others involved, things are complete. At this very moment, I am working on a business deal with three people involved. They all have the same name, but they are not blood relatives.

When the 88 days came around, the Visitors were there with me like clockwork. There were several days, maybe a week of visits from Them. These visits started on the 88th day just as promised. I had been having a pain that felt as if I had an abscess in my lower abdomen. It had plagued me since a previous surgery. There was a tremendous amount of healing of this problem during these visits, and the pain was cleared up.

Each day during this time, I would wake up with a knowingness that I had much more ability to know about anything that I needed to know. It is kind of hard to explain, but when I would open my eyes, I knew that I was more enlightened and that I could see into forever and know everything more strongly than usual.

It usually dissipated to some degree as the day wore on, but there was always a certain amount of knowingness that remained. I was like a sponge. I could only take in so much at a time. When I was overloaded with energy, some of it seemed to fall by the wayside.

The healing made me think about friends of mine that were in need. Now that I am looking back, I find it interesting that I have had so many friends in my life over the years that were paralyzed. Some were paralyzed before and some were paralyzed after I met them due to accidents and other causes.

Cindy was one of my friends who were paralyzed before I met them. She lived in Atlanta. After I had done my sessions with Van, I convinced her to come and see him for a session. Of course, my motive was obvious, but Cindy had been very determined over the years that she was going to walk again but not with anyone else's help. She was convinced that she could do it alone.

That didn't deter me. I wanted her to do it my way, because she had not yet accomplished her goal. She agreed to make the drive with me to see Van.

When she got on the table to get her reflexology treatment, it wasn't long before Van looked up from his work in surprise. He said, "Jesus is standing beside you, Cindy. He wants you to get up and walk." I was elated; my plan was working, but my heart quickly sank when she replied, "No, I want to heal myself. I will do it my way." Again, there is that free will, and it was not her will or her way to be healed then. She got her way and I didn't, but I understood that it was her choice to make, not mine.

I had spent my time with Van and done some lectures on my encounters and earth changes in North Carolina and decided that it was about time to move on. It was nearing winter time, and the dreaded cold weather was coming soon.

I felt there were a couple of other things that had to be done before I left, but I didn't know what they were. I also felt prompted to move on because I had a vision of the area where I was living: the top of the mountain behind my house fell off right before my eyes. Even though I was shocked to see this, I felt that I was safe for now, and it wasn't quite time to leave North Carolina yet.

I was then guided to prepare a lecture and go to Atlanta to give it. While I was in Atlanta, I decided to get a psychic reading with a lady named Patricia. At the time, I had totally forgotten about the Visitor that came to me while I was waiting for Paula in the car at Lowe's that one day.

I was surprised during the reading when Patricia mentioned the situation about my move to North Carolina and my main purpose there. She said, "You received a message one day that said you would meet a man who would help you." I flashed back to that day in the Lowe's parking lot.

Patricia went on to say that my main purpose in that area was with this man who did body work, and she mentioned that he was truly enlightened.

It was strange that I had never put two and two together about the message I received in the car that day and Van. Duh! Of course, it makes sense now, and from what I know about that relocation to North Carolina, meeting Van was the key to everything that transpired there on the greatly needed spiritual and soul level.

If Patricia had never mentioned this to me, I don't know if I would have realized what had just happened in North Carolina and how important my Visitor and Van were to me. My life's path was truly guided. I now know that Van had helped me in many ways. I wondered why it had taken this woman for me to realize that Van was the person I was to meet when it should have been so obvious to me.

Over the years, I have gotten a lot of similar quick messages from the Visitors that have paved the way for me to follow a certain path, but I didn't recall a lot of these incidents until I started writing this book eons ago. Thank goodness I kept a running notebook and audio tapes about each time I received them.

I was truly thankful for Van's assistance in all that had transpired during my time there. I begrudged having to leave Orlando so soon. I know how important that time in Orlando was for me, but I also know and understand more now about the whole purpose of going to that area of North Carolina. Paula was the instrument, and I am truly grateful for the entire experience. I don't know about the timing, but maybe it was crucial for my health to relocate at that time. I guess I don't have to know everything; I will just follow the guidance.

Besides Van, I met another man in the mountains that I almost forgot about. He did help me, but I didn't follow through very well. I was guided to meet him and was given his full name and then led to where he was. I actually had several meetings with him. His name was Peter.

For the sake of saving a tree, I will be brief about Peter because it is a very long story. Before I met him, I was told that I should go to him and do time travel. I knew nothing about time travel or if it was even real. Peter had been in contact with various species from other planets for years and was better at following his guidance than I was.

During my initial meeting with Peter, we had a long discussion about alien contact. Everything I said to him about my encounters and everything he said to me about his encounters was identical. After an hour or so of this back and forth, exact-experience conversation, he said that he understood why I was led to him, and that we should pursue some work together with time travel. He had a lot of the knowledge and equipment to be able to do this, as he told me.

Long story short, I did try to go through with it, but I was too scared of the unknown. A lot transpired that day, but I did not complete the time travel. I guess I should rephrase that by saying that I wouldn't allow it to happen. I was not familiar with his work and was concerned about the unknown. I see now that many things in my life would have been much better had I followed through with those plans.

There are never enough hours in my life to pursue all of the guidance that I get. Earth time is not the same as being in a space where there is no such thing as time. This guidance comes from a space like that; therein lies my problem. The messages and events happen so fast, I can barely keep up. In addition to that, I am too detail oriented in everything I do, which is time consuming.

I experienced several hardships during this time in North Carolina. Most of the time, I certainly didn't feel as though I were having a day at the beach, as far as happiness goes. My finances were not good and that is a great handicap. However, it was a time for progress spiritually and physically, which is much more important than money.

One night, I made myself a bed on the floor. My head was right next to the five-foot-tall, copper pyramid that I often sat under to meditate. Just as I lay down, I kept getting a thought, over and over again. I thought about what a psychic friend in Orlando had said to me. She told me that my problem with financial progress was that I had more desire to help others than to help myself. She also said that Jesus wanted me to have a new home, so I would be more comfortable and have no subconscious worry about it, which would allow me to work more easily.

With those thoughts continuing, I got the feeling that I should quickly lie down. I was sure that something was getting ready to happen. Just as I got comfortable, there was an intense, Christ-like energy at the top of my head. It started moving down to about the thigh area and stopped. It stayed in that exact position for about fifteen minutes. Then, I received a telepathic message, "Yes, it is important, and I do want you to have a new, comfortable home, and I will see that you get it." I was really surprised by this.

Just then, I remembered that my friends had often said to me, "Why don't you ask questions or for more information when you have a visit like this?" My logic said this was my chance. I quickly asked, "How much am I supposed to spend for this home for myself?" Then came the biggest shock; the answer was a huge dollar amount, huge to me anyway. The message continued, "It is important for you to be more comfortable and at peace."

There was a lot more to the message, but the main thing I remember was that a healing process was taking place as well as an energy transfer.

I have always felt that it was more important to help others than myself, but I guess at times, I have gone a little overboard. It is hard not to when you have compassion for others. It is more blessed to give than receive.

My willingness to help others is out of compassion. No matter how bad I think my finances, health, or anything is, I can always rid my thoughts of my so-called problems by looking around to find someone who is worse off and if possible try to help that person in some way. I have always been taken care of in every way. Many times, miracles have come along and helped me with my finances just when I needed it.

Money always helps, but it's really all about the spiritual journey and not about the material things.

Again, *I thanked God for being Chosen.*

Chapter 8
The Star in the East: Mystery Solved

I was about to receive several blessings as I entered another phase of my life. Even after all of the strange events that occurred in the North Carolina Mountains where I lived with Paula, I was going to receive some truly unexpected and shocking information.

I was about to learn one of the secrets—an omission from the Bible, an answer to one of the mysteries of the ages—and learn more about why I am involved with the Messengers.

Paula's decisions changed my life again. She decided to move farther north in the Carolinas to be near a friend that was like a sister to her. This left me all alone in a place where I saw no prospects for making a living. I was now going to have to make another sudden residential move just like when Sue got married. I wondered why all of this was happening to me.

I reflected on the recent changes in my life and realized that things had to change for me in the financial department. I realized that I definitely needed to be more independent. I also recognized how beneficial my volunteer work had been to me. Not only had I spent a lot of time on it, but I had been involved with two different spiritual missions that I saw as learning experiences with benefits. Those two missions were with Jim and the actor's seminar. The few days that I had spent with speaker were short; however, my time spent as the manager of Jim's seminars was quite lengthy and time-consuming with all of my varied duties and the travel involved.

Reflecting on this work seemed to usher in the much-needed guidance for my future missions. As I sat in my living room dwelling on these thoughts, a Messenger popped in with new instructions for me. He telepathically told me that it would be beneficial for me to do a television show with *Unsolved Mysteries*. I contacted them and told them a little about my encounters. At the end of the conversation, we agreed upon doing a show together.

I spent considerable time over a period of a few months in helping one of their producers put a show together that would tell of only a small segment of my life. At that point, I did not have the big picture yet. However, the smaller picture was amazing enough to interest them.

When we neared the end of the project, I learned that the producer was going to be going on a leave of absence from her job for a few months. I was asked to put all of this on hold until she returned. After those few months had passed, I had so much going on in my life that I didn't have the time to devote to the show. It was another one of those learning experiences for my future. I now knew a lot more about preparing a show of this type, but I had just been getting my feet wet for a long journey.

Another television production company contacted my attorney about doing one of their shows. When we got to the fine print, it was obvious that they basically wanted to own me and my life for a small fee. I, of course, turned it down.

My next instructed mission was to do lectures in Atlanta. It snowballed and I gave the lectures in Orlando and North Carolina, too. A small portion of the lectures were about my life with the Messengers. Also included were the coming earth and societal changes, as shown to me by Them, and preparedness tips for the time when these future events would come to pass. Many years have passed since then, and I have witnessed a large number of these changes occur just as I had been shown. Fortunately, a few of the worst events that were shown to me have not yet come to pass and hopefully never will.

After the public appearances, I was invited to do lectures in other parts of the United States. One of those invitations came from a New Age event promoter in Albuquerque, New Mexico. I did several projects with her that led to my going to Boise, Idaho, with Paula, who had then become my manager.

I was also invited to come to Gulf Breeze, Florida, to do a lecture and a radio show. The show was going fine until we got near the end of it. The guy doing the interview became a real jerk and said something sarcastic about my experiences. He abruptly cut my microphone off after his comment. It sounded as though he was trying to derail the lecture. His comments did not hurt the turnout at all, though. It went great. After all, it was Gulf Breeze; what did he expect?

All of this was very interesting and purposeful but were not things that I felt that I should make money from since it was spiritual work. I charged only a minimal fee to cover the expenses. I had various other assignments in the same vein but I still barely made enough to cover expenses due to my small fee. After a while, I was reminded that people do need to be paid for their time, even if it is spent on spiritual concerns.

Becoming more spiritual caused me to be more compassionate about the needs of others. As I mentioned earlier, I had gone from living a materialistic, socially conscious life to a more peaceful, spiritual lifestyle. I think this is a normal process in life. I have no regrets about the volunteer work I did, because I know I helped a lot of people. That was my mission.

One day, I sat down again and flashed back through all of the nonprofit experiences that I had been through. I found myself feeling an urgency to move on with my life. I guess I was really anxious about my circumstances, because as much as I hate cold weather, I called Paula and asked her to find an apartment for me that was near her. I chose the closest move that I thought I could afford to make in order to be closer to a friend. Paula found a very nice apartment for me, almost next door to her.

I immediately sold a number of my personal belongings to make this transition and never looked back. I knew more changes were in process, but I was totally unaware of the scope of these changes that were about to take place, changes that were worth more than money. As it turned out, the move was the right decision, because a huge coincidence was about to occur.

After I made the choice to move near Paula again, I learned that Sue was also moving to that same town; believe it or not. We had all left Orlando, scattered to other areas, and then came back together in this small town in the mountains at very close to the same time. After learning that Sue was going to be living nearby, I gave a sigh of relief and felt a lot better about my life. I felt sure that I was on track with my guidance, and that I had been given this blessing.

Paula was a friend who led me to a lot of situations that I needed to be in, just as I did for her. Again, I guess this is all fate and the way things are meant to be, even though I have questioned some of the changes I have been led to. At this point, I try hard to go with the flow and allow them, even when I am not happy with what is happening.

Now that I had my new home settled near friends, I decided to go back and forth to Atlanta to do more lectures. Just about the time I made that decision, I awoke to find that I wouldn't be doing any traveling. As I looked outside, I saw that my car was almost buried in snow. Instead of traveling and working, I would be getting a restful break.

This was a rare treat for me, not the snow but the time on my hands considering that I always had something that had to be done and it usually needed to be done yesterday, at least by my standards.

My meditations had been neglected with all of the changes going on in my life. Since I wasn't going anywhere for a couple of days, I decided to use my time wisely by meditating. Thank goodness I was snowed in, because I was about to get more clarity on some of my past bizarre experiences.

I barely got settled in my chair to meditate when an Entity, one of the Messengers with a high spiritual vibration, appeared in my room. He started speaking to me telepathically. He was loud, clear, and emphatic as He said, "Call Doctor John Mack at Harvard and do it now." I immediately called directory assistance to get his phone number. I had learned from past experience that I should act right away when a message comes to me with this kind of urgency or is that emphatic.

Prior to this event, I had been instructed to contact Doctor Mack and another professor at the Massachusetts Institute of Technology. I didn't contact either one of them at the time. I didn't want my life turned upside down by giving my information out to the public. I was still hiding my life, even from most of my friends. I chose to avoid these high-profile professors like the plague, so I filed the information away with my book notes and did nothing about it at the time.

I had heard that Doctor Mack was a professor at Harvard, a psychiatrist, an alien researcher, an author, and a Pulitzer Prize winner, but I didn't know anything else about him. I assumed that I would be like a Jane Doe to either professor. I didn't think that they would truly believe in aliens or UFOs. I was concerned that their purpose might be to debunk alien encounters. I had seen various debunkers on television shows. I am no longer concerned about debunkers; I now see them as people who are still working from that flat-world theory.

None of that really mattered at that point, as I had been instructed to call Doctor Mack for the second time. I called his office and spoke with his assistant, Pat. I felt quite brave as I told her specifically and honestly why I was calling. I even told her how the Entity had visited me in my room for the purpose of instructing me to call him. I explained that this had been my second request to make this call, but that I had previously ignored it.

I was quite surprised to hear Pat say, "That is very interesting." I actually expected her to call the men in white coats; after all, Doctor Mack was a psychiatrist.

I went on to explain to Pat that I didn't know why I was supposed to talk to him. I told her that I knew he was dealing with these kinds of matters, but that I didn't know what his position was on them. She explained to me that he did alien research and regressions for experiencers, as she called them. I got the impression that he was a believer from the way she spoke about it, but I wasn't sure.

Pat explained that she would tell him about my call, but she wasn't sure I would ever get a call back from him because he gets dozens of calls just like mine.

As I hung up the phone, I felt as though I had done my part and hoped that whatever was meant to be would come out of this contact with his office, so I settled in again for meditation. Just as I began to relax, the phone rang. It was Doctor Mack returning my call. He was very enthusiastic about the subject matter, which made me feel a little more comfortable.

He asked me where I lived. He was surprised when I told him the area of North Carolina that I lived in, because he was going to be at a seminar near my home in a few days. He seemed to be amazed and excited at the manner in which I had been told to call him, so he decided that we should meet. He set up the time and location to meet with me. He said that he would do an interview with me first. If he felt that my experiences were authentic and of interest for further pursuit, he would do a regression with me.

I had previously tried a couple of regressions with other hypnotherapists that were not well-known. Those regressions didn't work at all. That disappointment caused me to underestimate John's technique and ability. My previous track record with guidance had been good, so I went on faith alone even though I was still a little skeptical about the meeting. Would I be in control of what was happening if he decided to do a regression? Would I remember what I recalled in a regression?

With these fears in mind, I called my friend Barbara who happened to live near where I was to meet with Doctor Mack. I asked her to go with me, just in case he did a regression. She was very excited to be able to meet him and witness whatever was going to take place.

As soon as I shook hands with Doctor Mack, I was truly impressed and felt comfortable with him in person, as I did on the phone. A short time into our conversation, I could tell he was very open-minded and a genuine person. He handled everything as a matter of fact, which surprised me. Early in our meeting, he told me that he preferred I call him John. He was truly a humble man and knew who he was.

He skipped most of the seminar that he was in town for and spent the time with me. He conducted a very professional interview that lasted a few hours. He then brought in a couple of women to sit in on the second half of our interview. These ladies lived nearby and did clinical work on these same issues. Both ladies seemed rather impressed with what I had told them about my encounters.

After a visit with these clinical workers, John dismissed them and prepared to do my regression. He was so excited at the possibilities that might be uncovered by a regression after the interview. He allowed Barbara to witness it and take notes. He and I both audiotaped the entire day's conversation and the regression. John also signed an agreement that had been prepared for him in advance that covered several issues. One was that I would be allowed to divulge information about our meeting in any manner that I chose. My Guides advised me that I should protect myself by covering some of these bases since they wanted me to publish a book in the future. After I met John, I really didn't feel that the document was necessary, but it was prepared and he didn't mind signing it. It seemed that he and I were on the same page, so to speak.

Before I went into the regression I asked John to please refrain from asking me anything about the Greys. In our earlier conversation, I had told him about my encounters with them. Those encounters were initiated when I was wide-awake and in an alert state, sometimes even when other people were present.

I had heard negative as well as positive stories about the Greys from other people. If I had experienced anything with them other than my waking encounters, I didn't care to know about it. I only wanted to uncover the important things about my encounters and didn't want to be traumatized. John understood.

The preliminaries were finished so we got down to business. John started the regression with his method of relaxation. Within a couple of minutes, I felt comfortable and very relaxed. He then proceeded to take me into a deeper hypnotic state. It seemed as though I was deep in the regression within a couple of minutes.

I quickly started seeing and feeling events as if they were actually happening in the moment. One of the most amazing and important events that I relived seemed to be from one of my past lives. I was inside a body that felt as though it was mine. I felt a robe or some kind of fabric draped around my body that touched the top of my feet. I stood there watching the events that were going on around me.

I was being distracted by the fabric touching my feet, when all of a sudden; I looked up and to my right just in time to see Baby Jesus handed to Mary. He was wrapped in what appeared to be a blanket. As this event unfolded, I could see a few other people standing there too.

Just after the baby Jesus was handed to Mary, my attention was drawn to the eastern sky. I looked up to see a huge object that shone brightly. I stood there gazing at it, expecting to see nothing but the stars. Evidently, my thoughts were read because I heard a voice say telepathically to me, "That bright light in the east is not a star; it is our spacecraft."

The bright light, Their craft, was hovering nearby in the sky while other people were still with Mary. Some of the people in the group standing around with us were Light Beings. I was made aware that those Light Beings had come to Mary in that spacecraft. They were the same ones that communicated with me at that time. I knew these Light Beings were Jesus's People from the place of his origin.

I don't know how I was involved in this situation, other than that I knew I was somehow a part of all that was going on. I stood there and watched the event unfold with Joseph, Mary, and Jesus.

John was amazed at what I was reliving, but he wanted to keep moving into other areas of my past. He moved along faster than I preferred to, as I wanted to stay there and learn more about Jesus and myself.

Each event that I relived made me want to stay in that space and time. I felt that each one was educational, but I was also just curious about them. I don't know if it is true, but I have heard that you can get stuck in the past while doing a regression. Possibly that is why John was moving me along so fast.

He proceeded along by asking me what happened with me around the age of five. I quickly said, "Wait... wait, I'm being born right now." I could feel myself going through the birth process and knew that I couldn't breathe. I don't recall if I mentioned that to John at the time. I was aware of a couple of Messengers in the room where I was born. They were positively God-like Light Beings, not people from Earth. I wasn't aware of anyone in the room except for my mother, the doctor, and these Beings. I have no way to know if anyone else in the room saw or sensed Them.

All of this was so real in the regression; it was like reliving the detail and emotion in real time. I got more upset when I became aware that these Beings in the room with me were actually Beings that I was connected to with my soul body, for lack of a better word. I felt a bond with Them and knew They were a part of me, as if family from elsewhere. I also knew that I was incarnating into a body right here on Earth, and that I was from the same place that They were from. I knew beyond a shadow of a doubt that these were *my People* because of my feeling of connection with Them. I wasn't fully separated from the knowledge of where I had come from or who They were at that point. I was still partially living in my spirit body.

I also instinctively knew that these Beings were going to leave Earth and leave me here. This awareness during my birth caused me to panic about the situation, and I was still having trouble breathing.

These Beings were able to do something to my heart or lungs, it was like imparting energy, and then I started breathing. I knew at that point that They had saved my life. The worst part was knowing that I couldn't do a thing to stop Them from leaving without me. I became more frightened at the prospect of being in this new place with total strangers. It was traumatic for me, and I felt helpless.

As I was reliving all of this, I was also aware that John was trying to talk to me. He asked questions, but I was stuck reliving my birth and wasn't really paying much attention to him. I wanted to see what was going to happen to me next. At that point, I was very emotional. John kept asking me what was going on, but I couldn't speak. I was all choked up from the tears I was holding back. I was embarrassed that I was having this emotion in front of a stranger. Finally, I couldn't control it any longer, and I started to cry.

When I was finally able to speak, I told John what I was experiencing. He was so compassionate and tried to comfort me by saying, "If these are your People, and if They have saved your life, why is that so sad?" I explained that I was so sad because I wanted to be with Them, the only people that I knew at that time. I explained the scary emotion I was feeling about the fact that I would be left with all of these strangers and be so defenseless.

I now know beyond a shadow of a doubt that these Beings are from the same place that I had just come from; They were definitely my People. It was extremely traumatic for me to be abandoned at that time, although it was very cool to have my People there with me for a short time anyway.

I experienced a number of additional things in the regression, each one eventful and purposeful. The two major highlights for me were the experience of having seen Jesus's birth and my birth. It was interesting that my People were at my birth, just as Jesus's People were at His birth. While I was at His birth, I felt a part of His People as They were speaking to me. All of this made me wonder if my People and Jesus's People are one and the same or if there were two groups of Light Beings present at that time. I had a gut feeling that we all had the same purpose on Earth, as crazy as that sounds especially given the time span.

When my regression with John finished, I was amazed at what I had uncovered, things that I was not aware of prior to it. I also had an Aha! moment; it became clear that I had just learned the truth about the Star in the East. I now know beyond a shadow of a doubt that the bright star that was seen at the birth of Jesus was actually a spacecraft. That was truly amazing to me.

Through the regression, I also gained a lot of clarity about my encounters and learned more about my purposes in this life, all totally spiritual in nature. John was also amazed by the things we had uncovered. He did such a great job with me; he was a true professional.

At this stage of my life, I still have a hard time even thinking or talking about my birth experience, because it is just too painful. It was the most heart-wrenching sorrow I have ever had, worse than losing a loved one because of death. It makes me wonder if Jesus experienced these same feelings at His birth.

    I also wondered if Jesus came to Earth in a spacecraft, or if He had been born by the natural birth process with Mary while His People were there to make sure He was all right. I had turned around just in time to see Him being handed to Mary, which leaves me guessing about His actual birth process. Maybe I wasn't supposed to know about that right then, and maybe that is why I wasn't looking in that direction for the few seconds prior to it.

    After my birth, I had felt such negative energy from the new environment I was in. No offense to my mother at all; the negativity was not from her. I felt more a part of my People at that time than I did as a part of her, though. Earth would automatically feel negative compared with where I had just come from. No wonder babies cry when they are born; it was a very sad experience for me for sure. That also explains why there is a need for a bonding with parents and children at birth and thereafter.

    John later asked me if I knew whether it was an obstetrical fact that I had experienced a problem with breathing when I was born. It was in fact true; I was born a blue baby. My mother had told me about that when I was a teenager. She told me that I was born at home, and they were very concerned about my survival due to the breathing problems.

    Of course, the doctor removed the cord from around my neck, but the energy that was imparted to me by my People prior to that removal certainly saved my life; I could feel it happening. I was very aware of Them and what They were doing to me at my birth. I can see now that They had to be there to make sure I lived to fulfill a mission They had sent me on.

I just wish I knew the extent of the mission even now; I know I am not finished. I am obviously curious about it. They always give it to me in bits and pieces through each encounter and experience with Them. I can't see the big picture until I receive all the pieces of the puzzle.

One observation I have made is that I have lung and breathing problems that developed later in my life. I wonder if there is any psychological reason for this lung problem to have developed that might correlate to the problems from my birth. The body and the mind is an amazing machine.

The fact that I can even relive past events in a regression is very bizarre to me. Regressions are strange; you go through a wide range of emotions. At first, you are very happy, and then suddenly, you can be going through an experience that is truly frightening or sad. This can switch in a split second. It feels like the entire regression lasts only a few minutes, when in fact, it could have been hours.

Barbara observed an interesting thing as she sat at the end of the bed where I lay for the regression. She could see an energy that looked like heat waves the entire time. The waves were shimmering just above my body. John and I both experienced a noise that sounded like a train that went right through our heads at the end of the regression. We were surprised that we both experienced the same thing. It was as if the energy that Barbara saw passed through us.

When I see little children on television ripped from their families, the only people that they know, for one purpose or another, I have a flashback to the day I was abandoned. I feel their pain and my pain all over again.

After the session with John was complete, he expressed to me that he felt my experiences in the various encounters had given me the ability to heal others. I was surprised to hear him say that. I had never thought of myself as having that ability. Of course, I knew that he meant the healing would be done through me and not by me.

I had often wished for the ability to heal others. I assumed that I would have been told about it if it was to be. I have had a couple of people tell me they were healed from a particular ailment after they had been in my presence. In addition, my dad called to tell me that a tumor on his hand had been healed due to my presence. He had shown it to me while I visited him. When I left that day, the tumor disappeared. He insisted that he knew I was the reason for its disappearance. He had previously undergone surgery to remove it, but it returned again. After this disappearance, it never returned. I had passed all of these remarks off, since I couldn't relate them to having anything to do with my presence.

Others have said that after sitting in meditation with me, they felt calmer from my energy and they didn't want to leave my presence and go back into their hectic world. I have attributed that to the spiritual state that I shift into when I meditate and/or possibly due to the fact that my Guides were present at that time. I still have the desire to heal people at some point in my life, if it is meant to be.

Thank God for John Mack. He was so helpful to everyone that he came in contact with regarding encounters with aliens. He was the first person who truly helped me put the pieces of the puzzle together in my life. I later heard stories that he planted information in the minds of his regression clients that caused them to have a specific recall through a false memory. I find it hard to believe that he actually did this. My experience with him was the total opposite. During my regression, John had wanted me to go back to my childhood, around the age of five, to see what I was doing then. I didn't go to age five; I immediately went to the time of my birth. This says it all to me.

Prior to the regression, I had told John that I felt as though my encounters began way back at an early age. He said that a lot of people who experience alien encounters have learned that their encounters started around age five. I don't know if that was his reasoning for asking me what was going on with me at that age.

I later spoke with another well-known author and experiencer, at one of his lectures regarding his alien encounters and also found him to be very helpful and encouraging. I needed courage to write this book and to talk about what has been happening in my life. He said to me, "You are telling the truth as it actually occurred, so don't be afraid to tell your story." I thanked him for that comment as it helped me proceed with the book to bring my story to the public. Without John Mack, I don't think I would be writing this book today. I give thanks for him very often.

It is so difficult to live in a reality that isn't like the reality of other people around me. I used to be concerned about people believing my life story, especially the alien encounters. I finally decided that it doesn't matter what others believe. What they believe will never alter what has happened and is happening in my life. My visits and encounters will go on and on without anyone's permission or belief. I only answer to a high power.

I had done quite a bit of public work but I didn't realize that I had done enough at that point for it to actually be noticed. I later found that someone was paying attention. I happened to open the book titled *Abduction* by Doctor Mack, which he had sent to me as a gift. I was surprised to find that he had autographed it. For some reason, I had not noticed this before. He had written, "For Jenna, who has helped so much to make this reality known." He signed it, "Warmly, John." He was still being his humble self. I was very grateful for his generosity and comment. At that time he was speaking about my public lectures regarding encounters in general, as opposed to the new reality that I now speak of in this book.

I really appreciated that he took the time to let me know what he thought about my work. That was the way he was with all of us. His view of this work was that we were all in this together, and he realized that each individual played an important role. My role and my experiences are in creating a new reality for the world as well as for me. This is a benefit and a great gift for mankind. I am living in this true reality and so are the nonbelievers. A lot of them just don't know it yet.

After my initial meeting with John, I continued to be in touch with him for various reasons. We had several meetings over the phone and in person regarding new things that were happening in my life. One day, he called to ask if

I would like to do his book tour with him. I, of course, consented. I wanted to return a favor to him, as he had graciously helped me so much. He had teamed up with me with no reservations.

His tour included several national television shows. My first call to appear with John on television was from the producers of the *Oprah* show. Later on, some of his other subjects backed out of doing that show. They didn't want to go public for fear of wrecking their lives. I was game but didn't know what I was bargaining for, because I had not been on such a large television show before regarding this subject matter.

Oprah turned out to be the most real person out of all the television hosts that interviewed John and his subjects. She was very interested and seemed to believe in what was told to her about the encounters. I would say she is a very intuitive, spiritual woman; that was why she could relate to all of this.

A close friend agreed that I should go, even though I was hesitant for all the same reasons as Doctor Mack's other subjects. On the day of the show, some of them finally got up the nerve to speak publicly. This left me to speak only if I chose to volunteer.

The night before the *Oprah* show, we all met for dinner. I was introduced to some of John's other subjects at that time. I was quite surprised that I recognized some of them, even though we had never knowingly met. Strangely enough, the same ones recognized me as well. It was as if we were long-lost friends.

This show was much more powerful and emotional than I thought it would be. During it, they played a tape of one of John's subjects. It hit me emotionally as I picked up on his feelings. It was horrifying for to me to hear him going through pain with a Grey. I could barely keep it together through the show, so I didn't offer any comment on my experience. At that point, all of this was just too emotional. I glad that I didn't speak about my issues or my regression with John, due to all of the emotion going on during the show.

I wasn't prepared for the emotion I felt when I heard other people describe their encounters. It seemed to trigger flashbacks to some of my experiences, even though none of mine have been abusive or physically damaging that I know of. If anything like that has gone on, it would have been with the Greys, as they are known for that. Mostly, the other subjects' experiences triggered emotions associated with my own homesickness. That homesick factor, a feeling of being separated from loved ones, is a common issue I have spoken with other abductees about. It was especially strong for me since I learned that my People had left me here at birth.

There were other television producers who flew in to meet with me to discuss my being a part of their show. I soon found that most of the shows were not interested in learning anything or hearing the good things about abductions with visitors from other realms or planets. What they wanted was doom and gloom and somebody scared out of their wits. After I told them about my encounters, they politely informed me that I could not talk about anything spiritual during the interview. They didn't want to hear about alien encounters being related to anything spiritual. As far as I was concerned, that cut me out right there. I refused to leave out the spiritual aspect of the experiences as this was the most important reason for the experiences to begin with. I have always been a tell-it-like-it-is person, and I stick to that.

I was relieved after I walked away from those types of television programs. They miss the best and most important part, but I am sure they are only interested in boosting their ratings by focusing on trauma rather than educating the public. They miss the whole point of encounters, but a lot of them just work for the dollar. Doctor Mack often did interviews in which he talked about spirituality. I just assumed that he didn't mention it up in the original interview before the show.

When I decided that I would write this book, I called him to ask for a quote for it. I also wanted to get his impression of my experiences after the regression and of the other conversations and meetings that we had. He consented to an audiotaped recording of his quote over the phone. I personally feel that my encounters and regression experiences are best summed up by the following quote from Doctor Mack:

After meeting with Jenna and performing a regression on her, it is my opinion that her experiences of alien encounters are authentic. Her encounters are less common because they have been with various intelligences, such as humanoid Light Beings, and not limited to the Greys. Jenna's encounters have had a powerful impact on her spiritual evolution and sense of her own power. They have allowed her to discover capacities for healing and being of service to other people.

Doctor Mack was truly dedicated to his work and his subjects. He was always there for all of us when we needed him, and he was truly a special person.

The reliving of my birth experience occurred again a few years after the regression with Doctor Mack, when I was all alone. I learned a little more about the day of my birth. In this particular experience, an energy was transferred to my body that manifested itself in a totally different manner than normal.

The energy transfer created a delayed event, instead of the normal, immediate experience. I am not sure what type of process occurred at that time or if it was just a coincidence that I relived it again after the energy transfer. The good thing was that this time there was no interruption while I relived my birth, and I was able to gain more information about it.

The transfer took place one night as I was about to fall asleep. I felt the familiar presence of my People; They always come to me on the right side of my body. I felt an intense energy touch the right half of my head and my shoulder area. It is the kind of energy that makes your flesh tingle and your hair follicles stand up. I waited in anticipation for a new message, new instructions of some sort, or a healing. Nothing more happened, and then the energy went away.

I was puzzled but went to sleep and didn't think any more about it until I was awakened at 5:18 a.m. I then experienced myself being born and felt myself being very slippery. I saw the doctor that delivered me; he reminded me of Doctor Isadore Rosenfeld who does *Sunday Housecall* on television.

As I mentioned earlier, I knew that my People were right there with me as I was born. They were assisting with the energy that transferred to my body. This energy aided my breathing and bodily functions. After the transfer, I could feel my body start to work properly.

After the birth process was finished, I heard the doctor speak to somebody and say, "She came into the world about twenty minutes after the hour, as we were rolling in toward daybreak. We had a little trouble with the breathing, and she was blue. We got it all straightened out, and she is fine now." Then I heard another voice say, "What time was she born?" The doctor replied, "It was 3:20 a.m."

Then I heard my mom speak to someone in the room with her; she repeated the exact same words that the doctor had just said, as she told this person about what he had told her happened during the birth. Then she added, "The baby had been in danger for a while, but he was able to get her straightened out, and she will be fine." Obviously, my mom was doing fine, too, but I understood that my dad had fainted due to the smell of ether.

As the reliving continued, I was placed in the living room where my dad was. My mom was still in the bedroom. I wanted my dad's attention, but he wasn't paying attention to me as he appeared to be very ill and was sitting on the couch. Then our household assistant came into the room and tried to sit on Dad's lap. I was shocked by seeing this, so I snapped out of what I was reliving and found myself back in the present day.

I later recalled that my mom had told me a couple of things about that time of her life and my birth. She said that she later learned this household assistant was chasing after

Dad. She also told me that I had been born a blue baby. I never again thought about my birth after she told me all this, until it came up in the regression.

As I thought about my birth and witnessing the arrival of Jesus on Earth, I had an idea. It was about the section of the Bible that tells of the birth of Jesus. What if there was an error in translation? Maybe the word *star* should have been *light*. If so, then it would read Light in the East, not Star in the East. Maybe that is where the mix-up came in.

In the Bible, it says something like this: the star went before them until it stood over where the young child was. This indicates something moving that led them to where Jesus was born. To me, that tells it like it is.

There are so many people that have their own interpretation of that part of the Bible. I allow them their truth, but this is what I have been shown as a truth. Some interpretations have been things like an unusual star that was supernatural in nature. To some, it is and was a supernatural experience.

At Christmas, I hear the story told as if there were a bright star that led the wise men to where Jesus was born. It doesn't even seem logical to me that the wise men saw an actual star from a great distance and followed that star to Jesus.

I now know beyond a shadow of a doubt that the Star in the East was Jesus's People in a spacecraft. I know what I know because the Star in the East explanation came to me from an amazingly powerful and omniscient source that is pure love and balance. It was the same vibrational frequency as the Messengers. That power speaks for itself.

The message came to me loudly, clearly, and concisely, and when I know what I know, I am convinced.

I have read that some believe that more than three wise men were there to see Jesus at his birth. Some say as many as twenty. While I was standing there, I observed very few people at the birth. I would say that there were approximately five or six people there besides Joseph, Mary, and Jesus, and I was one of them. Oh, and of course, there was the hovering craft above them. I do not know how many Entities there were inside the craft. No information was given to me at that time pertaining to the occupants of the craft, unfortunately. What I do know beyond a shadow of a doubt is that they were Jesus's People.

After writing this chapter, a new thought popped into my head one morning when I awoke. It seemed to be a thought as opposed to a dictation, but when I have early morning thoughts that seem to unravel before my eyes, I feel pretty strongly about them. I cannot say it came from the Messengers because I was not aware of Their presence at the time. So with that in mind, I will just call it a thought, but it may be true. The thought was that you always hear people talk about the second coming of Christ. I felt that His second coming just might possibly be Him coming to Earth in a spacecraft. Time will tell.

It was such a great privilege to relive the time when Jesus was born. I also thank God for the ability to visit with my People as often as I do while I am still here on Earth. They come back to me frequently, so at least I now know beyond a shadow of a doubt that they didn't just drop me here and forget about me.

They have so much knowledge to share with the people of Earth, and I hope to continue getting information for those who are willing to listen.

I have always been very spiritual and grew up attending church. I am grateful for the Bible studies and the friendships that I had in church, but there were many missing pieces throughout those years. The story was incomplete for me. I am grateful that I have been able to relive all that I have in order to fill in some of those missing pieces. Life and religion make a lot more sense to me now with this new knowledge.

Yes, the Messengers are my People; and yes, I nearly always think of Them when I am in church.

Chapter 9
Witnesses

Cindy, my friend in Atlanta, knew I would be in town to do another lecture in the near future. She had asked me to arrive a few days early to house-sit for her while she was away. It was a great opportunity for both of us. It would give me some extra time to relax and prepare for my lecture.

When I was in Cindy's home, I could always count on having at least one bizarre event. She meditated a lot so there was always a good vibe going on around her home. I knew that I would enjoy my time there, but I didn't realize that this visit would be quite as eventful as it turned out to be.

I settled in very early the first night to read and meditate but fell asleep before I finished my meditation. I abruptly awoke the next morning to the sound of a female voice speaking to me. I shot straight up in bed and found that I was alone. I had been startled by the voice, because I was supposed to be alone in the house. I blinked my eyes a couple of times and looked at the clock to see that it was only 4:45 a.m.

After I saw that there was nobody in the bedroom but me, I quickly realized that the female voice was speaking telepathically. She was invisible to the naked eye, but I felt Her presence directly in front of my face at a close range. She had a kind and familiar energy. I felt as if I knew Her.

Her high-frequency, spiritual energy allowed me to know She was from a higher plane of existence.

By that point, Her intense energy was so close to me that I could feel it touching my body. I could almost feel a breath exuding from Her, although I knew She did not breathe in a physical sense. Her energy made my hairs feel like they were standing on end. I knew from past experience that something very spiritual was about to take place.

Suddenly, She manifested a pastel pink booklet that magically appeared out of thin air. It measured approximately 3 x 6 inches. She held the book in front of my face at a close enough range that I could see every word. She quickly turned the pages as She ran Her brown-skinned, slightly bony finger down the words on the page. Using Her finger as a pointer, She tapped on the words that She wanted me to read.

All of this was happening so fast that I couldn't digest every word. She kept tapping Her finger frantically on a name in the booklet as She said, "This is the mate of your soul." That name was Lee Harris. Strangely enough, I had already met this man twice right here on Earth and had an unusual encounter with him.

I was afraid that my Visitor was going to leave, so I quickly asked Her what Her name was. I don't recall if She pointed it out to me in the booklet or if She told me telepathically, but Her name sounds like Nasha. Nasha was still speaking to me telepathically. She told me that She is from the star of my origin. I asked Her what the name of this star is, and She replied, "Rising Star." I took Her statement to mean that I am from a place called Rising Star. I was glad to know the name of the place that I had originated from, as I had mentally asked that question many times. I was hoping to get an answer from my Guides.

After the fact, I questioned whether She meant that the name of it was actually Rising Star or if She meant that it was considered a rising star, as in astrology. However, in answer to my original question, She specifically told me that the name of the star is Rising Star. I don't know much about how astrology works, but I have heard that term used in astrology.

That same day, Nasha also said that the God-like Light Beings, the Messengers that have been coming to me from another planet are actually from the star of my origin. Her next words were, "They will be coming to take you home at precisely——." She gave me a time of day and date, but I can't find my note on this. I do recall that it would be dark when They came to get me, either at night or in the wee hours of the morning, but I don't recall the specific date.

I was concerned that someone would read my note, so I guess I hid it a little too well. I viewed this information as private and sacred and did not want anyone knowing about it.

At this point, I don't really feel that I need to know the date. I have faith, and I know beyond a shadow of a doubt that They will show up when the time is right, just as They always do. I am trying to live in the moment and allow the natural flow of evolution as well as allow and rely on Them to work in divine order.

I asked Nasha why She and the group from Rising Star had been coming to Earth. I had been privileged to see a lot of Their purposes, but I always assumed there was one larger event we were being prepared for that I didn't already know about. Her exact words were, "What is happening on Earth is nuclear fission, and We are coming to neutralize it." I will never forget hearing Her say that; it was such a shock to me. Sometimes, I feel that I should have asked more, but I felt that She would be leaving soon and time was short. I knew She had a purpose for coming to me, so I allowed Her the time to say what She needed to say.

Nasha merged consciousness with me for a short period of time before She left that morning. She did this by starting to speak to me telepathically, then in the middle of Her sentence it switched, and Her words started coming through my mind as if they were my thoughts. Then it switched back, and I was hearing the rest of the sentence from Her telepathically. This process was similar to an energy transfer. However, it did not have the intensity that the energy transfers have when penetrating my cells. It was merely a mental transfer of high vibrational frequency words that occurred seamlessly. It was not like a trance channel situation where an entity takes over your physical body.

The message that was transferred to my mind was something that I had no prior knowledge of; therefore, I knew that it came directly from Her.

Prior to this meeting with Nasha, a psychic had told me that I would be giving messages to the public in this exact manner—by mental transfer. Maybe someday I will be able to deliver messages from those on Rising Star in just that same manner. The process was actually effortless and pretty cool.

After the transfer had taken place, She departed with this last statement; speaking tearfully, She said, "I miss you." As She left, I felt very sad and homesick for Her and my People.

I recognized Her familiar energy; I truly did know Her after all. Her messages also resonated with my soul and provided a lot more information about my life.

On another occasion, Nasha spoke with me about my ability to know the future. She stated that this future information often comes to me through what is known as the River of Knowledge that exists in God's White Light. Based on my experience, when you are in the flow of the River of Knowledge, you automatically tap into things that are unknown as yet. You go out of Earth time and into the ether and a zone where time does not exist; everything happens all at once, everything just IS. If you raise your consciousness to the White Light level, then you can think of a question and get the answer through this connection to the higher frequency. When I am in a higher state of consciousness, I tap into the knowledge that exists in the White Light, which is connected to or is a part of God.

If you are in a higher state of consciousness, you would automatically attract information you need to know, unless you think of a specific thing or ask a question prior to raising your consciousness—in that case, you would receive the answer to the question. The secret to accomplishing this is to think of your question prior to going into your meditation. You can visualize it as making a connection through Wi-Fi with the understanding, of course, that you would be tapping into the expanded version of the Internet, what in reality is infinite wisdom.

You can also work to resolve issues in your life by dragging them into the White Light after you are there. It takes a lot of focus to forget about those issues while going to the Light and then to quickly pull them into the Light once you are there. With practice, it is possible.

Shortly after my visit with Nasha, I awoke one morning to another pleasant surprise. I had another Visitor; this time it was a male energy, one of the God-like Light Beings, in fact.

Right away, I heard a voice that started speaking to me telepathically. He said, "It was a beautiful landing on October 25, 1948, in a very remote area of Indiana." He also said, "Their mission on the day of that landing was to ensure that this messenger would live through the birth process," and then He vanished.

I thank God for my People and Their safe landing in 1948. I am also thankful for the opportunity to serve as Their messenger and accomplish the mission that I came here for.

I thought to myself, "Wow. He was talking about my birth date and location. He was so right; my birthplace was a very remote area, and as I had already relived my birth in the regression, I knew that They were there with me, and that They saved my life before Their departure from me. I was quite amazed with this statement since it fit right in with what I had recalled about my birth during the regression with Doctor Mack.

I had an uplifting feeling from the energy of This powerful male presence. In another way, it was very sad, because I still miss all of my People from Rising Star.

The thing that amazes me the most is the way They present each sentence. Each one is very profound, clear, concise, and articulate. The words flow in each statement as if they are poetry, even when they are not meant to be poetry.

They also have a way with poetry that is very melodic and can go on and on. I always wish that I could record Their words or at least remember all of the words to the poem. I usually cannot remember each word because the poems are too lengthy.

It seems that They have endless information to share, and I hope to be able to bring you more of it.

They have paid visits to me in numerous locations, but there were several visits in the Atlanta area. It has been great to have the friendship of and ability to share with my friend Cindy in Atlanta. She is so much fun to be around. Her house is certainly a hot spot for spiritual activity. I became even more aware of this fact while visiting her on another occasion.

I was in town to do a lecture at that time. As I was going over my notes for the evening lecture, I was surprised by an invisible yet powerful Visitor. I immediately received a telepathic message that instructed me to get the Bible from the bookshelf.

Once I had the Bible, the instructions continued. I heard the telepathic voice tell me to read from the Bible in the order dictated. I was told which book, chapter, and verse I was to read and even given the order that I was to read them in.

I had to jump around in the Bible in a hopscotch fashion to comply with the order in which I had been told to read them. Even though I was jumping all around in the Bible, the message ended up flowing perfectly and created a linear story of the events as they occurred.

I had always assumed that the Bible had been written in a linear time line, but it seems that I was definitely wrong about that, according to the way I had been instructed to read this information.

If I had read it in the linear order, as it is printed, the story would not have been in the proper sequence of the events that they were talking about.

A lot of what I read was about the story of Noah and the Great Flood. I asked why I needed to know this, and the answer was, "You were one of the sons of Noah." The message continued, "It is now time for your mission as Our spokesperson to include taking Our messages to mankind about becoming more self-sufficient and choosing a safe place to live."

These safe places are to be away from bodies of water, fault lines, and volcanoes. He went on to say, "This warning is to be much like the days when Noah warned people of their upcoming flood."

Of course, I had already had many visions of water flooding our planet in certain areas. This new message now made sense as to why I had been shown all of the past visions on earth changes, especially changes in certain areas of Florida where I had been spending a lot of time.

They also asked me to deliver a special message regarding the Holy Trinity, "The Holy Spirit is a person just like Jesus. He is on another planet." I had never heard that before, but I now know beyond a shadow of a doubt that this is a truth because I know the Messenger that delivered it.

It is so amazing to me that these things are actually happening on our planet in my lifetime: the visits, the messages and the actual changes. I am very thankful that I have been chosen to assist these God-like Beings.

Being thankful for being chosen opened up many adventures that I never dreamed of going on. In the past, I had volunteered to help with finding missing children many times. I had decided to move on to do other things but it seems I still had a calling for that. A couple of strange events happened that brought me back into it again for a short time.

One of these events happened when I was house-sitting for Cindy. When I arrived, I knew that she had already left for her trip. As I put my key in the door, the phone began to ring. Cindy knew the time of day that I was to arrive, so I figured she was calling to see if I got there.

I rushed to grab the phone only to find out that it wasn't Cindy. It was a stranger calling for me, a lady who had two missing grandchildren.

What were the odds of someone calling me at this number since I didn't live there and had not for a few years? I wondered how she made the connection to me at that phone number, so I asked her where she got it. She told me that the Atlanta police department gave it to her and recommended that she call me. I had assisted with a case there in Atlanta at one point in the past, so that finally made sense.

Another strange event happened that was very similar to this. One day, my mother called to tell me that she had a message for me. She said that someone called her number and asked her to pass it along. When this happened, she just thought that I had given out her number in case of emergency. However, that was not the case.

I called the phone number to ask the woman what she was calling about. She told me that she had a missing child and that she was told to call Jenna. I questioned her more, because I had never given out my mother's phone number for anything like this. Then I asked her to tell me the number she had dialed. When she repeated it to me, I learned that it was one digit off of my mother's number. She, in fact, had dialed the wrong number.

She had intended to call another person who had the same first name as mine. This other Jenna had helped with missing children also. The caller was so surprised by this turn of events that she decided I needed to help her.

Writing about all of these missions reminds me of Nasha's message to me about Lee Harris being my soul mate. I knew that he was on a spiritual mission as well. Since he is the mate of my soul, then he must also be from Rising Star. On another occasion one of the Messengers told me that I had a parallel life that lives here in the United States. I was given that person's name, so I know who it is, but they do not know me, yet. This person is a well know New Age speaker and has been for years.

I also wonder how many people there are from Rising Star that are here on Earth for a specific mission. I would like to meet Lee again as well as others from Rising Star. As I was wrapping up this paragraph, I telepathically heard a message, "It is time for a reunion." Now, I am excited at the possibility of such a reunion.

The first time I met Lee was at a lecture I was giving in North Carolina. He was an attendee there that evening.

When the lecture was over, a group of people flocked around to speak with me. He was one of the first people to introduce himself. Right away, I noticed that he had a high, spiritual frequency surrounding him, but I noticed it more at our second meeting. He introduced me to a book that he had in hand and wondered if I had read it. This was the second time a male friend had asked if I had read this same book. The Entity that channeled through Jim also mentioned that we should all read it; it is titled *The Keys of Enoch*.

I have to confess that I had been given that same book as a gift, and I still have never opened the book. After all of those hints from friends, I still have not read it. I guess I am supposed to mention this book now, since all of this information is coming to mind.

I decided to look it up on Internet. Here is what I learned: *The Keys of Enoch* is a textbook that states the issues of the future in spiritual and scientific prose and is known as The Book of Knowledge. The author is Doctor J. J. Hurtak and he has a video on You Tube.

At this point, I don't know why I am supposed to read it. Perhaps you may be led to read it after learning of it in my book. I am not endorsing the book, as I have not read it. I spend every spare minute that I have in writing this book. I have bought several books, but only for reading them when I retire.

Lee was very active in his spiritual work as well. I got the impression from others that he spends most of his time on a mission. My friend Cindy spoke of him as if she knew him or had met him.

He was lecturing at a new age expo in Atlanta when I met him the second time. This time, he saw me as I was mingling in the auditorium. He came right over to me with opened arms to greet me. When he got about three feet from me, I felt this intense, spiritual energy between us that was very powerful. It was so strong that I had a hard time getting close enough to give him a hug. In other words, there was a force field of energy that caused a cushion of energy between us. His first comment was, "Wow, I like your energy!" I told him that I thought it was his energy. We both laughed, not knowing what it meant at the time.

I have not seen him since. I have no idea where he lives now, but I recall that we had a phone conversation after the second meeting regarding alien encounters. At that time, he told me that he was moving to the upper west coast of the United States.

I didn't make the mental connection of what Nasha had told me about him being the mate of my soul until some years later while reading my notes. I either didn't know about it at the time of the meeting, or it had gone right over my head when Nasha told me about it. The latter is often the case when these Beings tell me things; I record the information and move on. I am always rushing off to the next thing, always too busy to see the forest for the trees. Thank God for notes.

I often forget about applying my time philosophy. That philosophy is that each day is the first day of the rest of our lives, and life goes on forever so there is no need to rush through it. I realize I should slow down and live in the moment a little more, and I feel like I will do that when this book is finished. I am very big on keeping my commitments.

I had another unusual experience with a girl at that same expo. She was casually walking by me when she abruptly stopped to read my name tag. She then asked if I was the same Jenna that was getting information from aliens regarding earth and societal changes to give to the public. When I said yes, she told me that she had also been having experiences with Beings from another planet.

She told me a story about a time when she had been visited by Them. While she was in Their presence, she was shown something about earth and societal changes. She then asked if she should help with getting that information out to the public. She swore that They had told her about me and that disseminating that information was part of my duties with Them.

She told me a story about how she was repeatedly having visions of a little boy. Every time she saw this same child, it was younger and younger. Then finally one day, she saw the child in a vision again. This time the child reached up to take her hand and said, "Hi, Mommy." That was the last time she saw the child, and the next thing she knew, she was pregnant. I thought her experience was pretty cool. These things never cease to amaze me.

That experience with the pregnant lady reminded me of an interesting friend named Bea. I met her while I was visiting relatives in Indiana. I felt as if I had known her forever; she was almost like a sister. We quickly became friends and spent time together while I was on this trip.

One evening as I was driving to the area where Bea lived, I spotted a very large, white light that was perfectly round; it looked like a ball of light but I could see it was an object. It was traveling at a fast pace just above the treetops. It suddenly slowed and went down below the trees in the vicinity of Bea's home.

While visiting with Bea, I told her what I had seen in the sky near her home. She acted as though she didn't want to discuss it. At that point, she didn't know about my encounters. She opened up to me a little more after I reassured her that I believed that some UFOs are spacecraft. She first told me that she had seen several UFOs that looked like what I described to her. She had seen all of them in the area of her home. I felt pretty sure that she knew more than what she was saying. Finally, I was able to coax her into telling me more. She admitted that she had witnessed a spacecraft landing years ago in Indiana, while she was traveling with her daughter.

When she saw this craft landing, she stopped her car alongside the road, along with a lot of other cars that had pulled over. She saw several people walking toward this ship. She didn't think she got out of her car, but she knew that she had missing time that night. After this experience, she began to feel a lot of spiritual guidance around her.

She later took a picture of an unusual cloud that was very similar in shape to a saucer-shaped spaceship. I saw her 8- x 10-inch photo and it looked identical to the photo of a cloud that was taken over Mount Shasta. I forgot whose picture that was, but it was made public.

After meeting Bea, I was starting to feel like I was a magnet for people who have had encounters with aliens or UFOs. I am sure there are some who have these encounters that we don't know about. They are most likely hiding as I did for years. For me, there were a couple of issues as to why I didn't want my experiences told to the public.

The biggest one was that my connection and visits with my People are a very personal, private matter. It is also hard to accept the fact that maybe I am a little different from other people. I guess we all want to fit in. Anyone who knows me will tell you that I have always been a very modest person, so bizarre events like these didn't seem like they could be happening to me.

After years of fascinating experiences and encounters, there came a time when I finally came to grips with the fact that I am actually on a mission here on Earth with these God-like Beings. As you likely understand, the reality of this is a difficult thing to come to grips with.

In the early years, I asked the question, "Why me?" At this point in life, I see things a little more clearly than I did then. I have had a chance to digest all of the information that I have learned. I now have the answer, and I know beyond a shadow of a doubt that I must go forward to the public with the full story. I am expected to share this story with the world; it is part of what I volunteered and was chosen for. This is who I am, and I accept it. The information is too important not to share with others.

After my time with Cindy and other friends in Atlanta, I was feeling a shift in another direction. I felt that I needed to get back to Florida to feel grounded for a while in order to get new instructions for my life's path. I always felt like Florida was my home base, even when I was a teenager. Atlanta was great during that last stay. A lot of unusual events occurred during my time spent there over the years, but I knew it was time for a change again.

I was led to call my friend Lynn who lived in Orlando. Lynn was a longtime friend who had a couple of properties. I asked if she had anything available for me. She didn't have anything right away but invited me to stay with her for a while until something became available. I took her up on her offer and it felt as though everything was going according to plan.

Lynn was another friend who was very intuitive and understood the metaphysical way of life. It was great to be back in her area and enjoy the balanced energy. We had a great time catching up, and it wasn't long before she has a property that I could live in. I moved into my new place and finally felt settled again.

My closest friends knew that I had an intuitive gift and accepted that as normal for me, but a lot of them did not know about my alien encounters. Some of these friends are in the entertainment industry, most of them are in music. Gene was a casual friend that I had met through my friend Rick, who was a musician. Gene didn't know anything about my encounters. I knew that he wasn't very open-minded about anything that he couldn't see or touch. All of that changed for him one evening at my home.

I bumped into Gene on the street one day and we had a brief conversation about his brother, John. He confided in me that he was very concerned about him. John had told him that he was having alien encounters and that these aliens were instructing him to meet them in various locations and that he had even been abducted by them. Gene thought that his brother had lost his mind, seriously. He just couldn't believe it because he didn't believe aliens were real.

I explained to him that I also had been having these types of experiences for years, and that John most likely had not lost his mind. Gene was shocked; he had known me for fifteen years or so and had never heard about this. He seemed relieved that I could vouch for the reality of aliens. We closed our conversation by setting up a meeting at my home. He was anxious to get validation for his brother's encounters by discussing the subject matter with me.

I arrived at my home after dark on the night of the meeting with Gene. I had to park behind my home to get to the front door. The minute I parked the car, I started getting this overpowering warning from one of my Guides, a warning that something strange and scary was about to happen. I had an overpowering feeling that I shouldn't get out of the car. I didn't understand why. Gene would be arriving soon, so I had to go in.

I tried to figure out a way to avoid the danger that I was being warned about. I felt very frightened each time I even thought about getting out of the car to go around the building on either side. My imagination went wild.

One end of the building was pretty dark, so I chose to go the other way and ran to my front door. I made it inside without incident. I quickly forgot about the fear once I was inside and saw that there was nobody in my home.

Gene arrived shortly, and all of the fear was forgotten. We sat down in the living room to chat. He sat across the room from me. My eyes felt really strained, and I was getting a headache. I thought it was because of the distance between us. I mentioned the vision problem to Gene only to find that he was having the same problem.

I seemed to be looking through energy waves in midair that were distorting my vision. I had never experienced that before; I didn't know what was going on. I soon felt a strong energy to my left side. My hair follicles felt prickly and electrified. I just ignored it all, because time was short, and Gene wanted to hear about alien encounters.

After a long-winded conversation about my encounters, Gene said that he really needed to go but wanted to hear more. Then he looked in the direction of the energy that I was feeling to my left and said, "I really do have to go now." He looked shocked, and his face was really pale. I asked him if he was all right. He abruptly said, "Somebody is standing in that corner." As quickly as it came out of his mouth, he was at the door and ready to escape.

I avoided looking in the corner as I asked Gene to describe what this Being looked like. He said, "He is wearing a long robe with a hood." I ask what the face looked like; he replied, "I can't make out the features as the hood is casting a dark shadow over the face." With that statement, he was out of there, still as wide-eyed and as pale as he could be. I closed the door and turned to look in the corner where I was still sensing the energy, but I didn't see a thing.

In all of my years, I have never seen or sensed an alien wearing a robe with a hood, but I took his word for it. It was pretty normal for me to have various alien Beings pop in unannounced. I had experienced past events that were similar to this when nothing more happened that I recall, anyway. Those Beings just watched and listened to the conversations that were going on with friends and myself. A few times, the other people in the room also saw these foreign Beings. That even happened when I gave lectures.

I ignored the whole event and proceeded to get ready for bed, although I did feel an urgency to get to bed quickly. As I entered the bedroom, I heard a telepathic voice say,

"Unplug your music bed before you lay down." The music bed is an electric, portable platform. It is the same size as a massage table and contains speakers that are strategically located to hit different chakras of the body as the music plays to enhance the quality of meditation. The bed that I slept in was a king-size bed that was two doubles together. I had the music bed on the opposite side of where I slept. I quickly pulled the plug and got into bed.

The minute I hit the bed, that same telepathic voice said, "Turn over on your right side." At that point, I could feel and sense a male alien Being standing beside the bed to my left. I didn't see a solid body; I sensed his presence and knew exactly where he was standing and I knew that he was approximately six feet tall.

I automatically turned over on my right side, as he was in command. He had caught me by surprise; there was no time to think. Instantly, a blanket of intense, electrical-type energy covered me from the top of my neck to the tips of my toes. It didn't touch my head, which was odd.

This energy was intense but a different kind of energy, one that I had never experienced before. The minute the energy hit my body, it penetrated every cell equally. This energy didn't stop once it had penetrated every cell of my body. That in itself was out of the norm for me. This whole process was different from anything that I had experienced before.

After this blanket of energy had fully penetrated each individual cell of my body, I could feel the entirety of my being/cells move down through the mattress and box springs. The process halted its motion just short of my cells hitting the floor. My cells were so close to the floor that I could actually feel the cold from the cement-slab flooring.

The cells were moving so forcefully through the bed that I thought I was going to go through the floor and disappear into the ground below the cement. With that thought, my cells suddenly stopped just short of hitting the floor. They stood in suspension for a few seconds, and before I knew it, my cells had come right back into my physical body.

While this process was going on, I could also feel my physical body separate from my cells. It was still lying on the bed like an empty shell, a motionless dead weight. It didn't feel like it belonged to me, but I could feel it lying there like a blob. I was definitely out of my body during this procedure. At that time, I was actually aware of both my spiritual and physical bodies at once.

When the force or intensity of whatever was being projected into my cells stopped its process, I slowly became whole and complete again after those tingling cells were back in my physical body. They seemed to automatically drift back upward and into my physical body until they were back in place. I suddenly realized just how many millions of individual cells our bodies consist of. Of course, the cells that I felt and sensed were actually my soul/spiritual body. My physical body still had its cells as it lay there on the bed as a solid mass. Our physical body is only a vehicle to house our soul. That is why my physical body lay there like a blob. It had no life without the soul.

Each and every cell had been saturated by this energy. I could still feel each cell tingling and vibrating with a high frequency after they were back in my physical body. It was as if an electrical charge had been applied to each individual cell. That sensation slowly dissipated equally from each cell, except for the fatty parts of my body, such as the buttocks. Those areas continued to tingle and vibrate with the electrical charge for a longer period of time. It took approximately five to ten minutes, if not more, before the tingling had stopped completely in most of my body. After those had calmed down, I could still feel the cells in the fatty parts of my body tingling for a longer period of time. I pretty much lost track of time due to being in such a daze over this whole thing.

I always feel calm and peaceful when the God-like Light Beings visit me for any purpose, especially when They do restructuring on me. This process was like a restructuring except for the bold, abrupt, and controlling attitude. It almost seemed like the process was removing something from my cells or revamping them in some way. Hopefully, he wasn't removing something that I needed or wanted.

It is possible that I felt he was abrupt because he took me by surprise; I thought he had left my house when Gene did. I'm sure you can relate to my fright; I was home alone and all of a sudden, a tall Being appeared beside the bed, right out of thin air.

After this bizarre incident, I was in a daze for several days. I was still terrified because this was out of the norm for me. I didn't even know who he was. All of my encounters may seem out of the norm to other people but up to this point most of them had been normal for me.

When this ordeal was over and I thought he was gone for good, I still didn't want to take any chances. To make myself stay wide-awake until morning, I used imaginary toothpicks to hold my eyes open. I barely took a breath or moved a muscle for the rest of the night. I still felt like someone was looking over my shoulder, even after I thought he was gone. It was probably my paranoia; after all that I had been through, I was very likely overly cautious.

I think the scariest part of the whole thing was that he had an authoritative attitude. I have never had an alien or Being of any type ever use an authoritative attitude with me; quite the opposite. That was definitely the scariest thing that has ever happened to me in my life.

I now call this alien The Intruder. He was definitely anything but welcome. This experience was worse than being held hostage, because he was semi-invisible. He had the ability to appear and disappear without notice by turning his frequency up or down at will to make his presence known.

I spent the next three days and nights without sleep. I was afraid of a return encounter with him. I was also afraid to leave my home; I didn't answer my phone or call anyone. I guess I was in a state of shock, dazed and definitely confused.

My afterthought was that leaving the building was what I should have done. Then I realized that I could be contacted in any manner, at any time or place by any of these Beings. I can't rationally explain any of my thoughts or actions at the time of this encounter. This was definitely out of the norm for me, as much as the other encounters had become the norm at this point.

After the third day of no sleep and staying in hibernation, I couldn't take it any longer. I decided to call my friend Leon. I knew he would understand and believe what had just happened to me. I had discussed alien encounters with him in the past. He had told me about a number of his personal encounters with alien Beings. He also explained to me that there are a huge number of Universal Light Beings visiting Earth at this time.

Leon said that he had never worried about anything they did to him, because the aliens were light years ahead of us in technology, and he figured they couldn't do anything but help us and our bodies.

At that time, I wanted him to come over to discuss what had happened to me. I felt like I didn't want to talk to him about my experience over the phone. I was afraid to go out of the house, and I didn't want to be alone for fear this same Being would come back. He thought I was being silly to worry about the encounter; he didn't think this encounter was that big a deal.

He had previously told me a bizarre story about how they opened up his back and did something to him as he lay in his bed. He just allowed it and was not concerned.

Leon stayed on the phone for a long time to comfort me. He explained how a lot of this kind of thing works. His efforts calmed my fears. After all, he wasn't afraid of his encounters, so why should I be? He also had a good point in that he felt that these Beings were light years ahead of us. After all, other than sleep deprivation, I didn't really have any other side effects.

I guess that comfort from a fellow experiencer was what I needed. I finally felt like I could get out of the house to eat and get back into society. That night after speaking with Leon, I slept for hours and hours.

I guess one aspect of this wild ride that I had just been on was a good thing. At least I had a witness to the visitor in the living room before Gene left. He is just one of several witnesses to my encounters. Witnesses in this line of work are always good, but I prefer to have had a witness that does not bring an entity along with him. I have no way to know for sure that this is what happened; however, I had never experienced anything like this before in my lifetime.

I have not told Gene about what happened after he left the house that night. I will bet that he would be afraid to be around me ever again, if I had told him.

There were no more encounters of any sort for quite a while. To this day, I still do not know why that happened. I could make a lot of guesses, but I have no real answers. I am sure I will be given clarity on this at some point. After previous encounters, I have been able to see what the purpose was but not with this one. All I can figure is that Gene had actually led this Being to me because of his brother's connection.

Gene told me that many times before and after our meeting, he has felt like someone is watching him. He feels they guide him also. I don't know if that is the good news or the bad news, but he thinks it's a good thing. The ones that are watching him may also be there to protect him from the one that blasted me that night. Who knows?

I do know beyond a shadow of a doubt that this encounter had nothing to do with my People from Rising Star. This goes to show you that there are many species that are actually visiting us. The good news is that this is the only time I have had that kind of experience.

I guess the lessons learned out of this are to stick with my assigned mission. I should not be getting involved with assisting others who are having encounters or those who want to learn from me on a personal basis about their individual alien encounters. That is not my role nor am I qualified for it.

After that experience, I often wondered where the mattress and box springs that I slept on that night ended up. Part of me is in them, but it might be a part that I would not want to get back.

If I had paid attention to the warning I was getting while sitting in the car, I most likely would never have had that experience. I didn't listen because I had made a commitment to Gene. I have always been dependable to a fault. He was a friend who asked for a favor.

I have a strange curiosity about that recent experience with the Intruder and have wondered if there could be some kind of territorial rivalry going on here on Earth or if all species visiting Earth are benevolent and working in a coordinated effort for our benefit. With all of our current pollution problems and the future issues that I am concerned about with our sun, I hope they are all working together. We have enough to worry about.

With that said, I know beyond a shadow of a doubt that The Nine are not territorial. However, They do protect me when I listen to Them. They have too much power to be concerned about having to protect Themselves from other species. They have the ability to take over everything if They so desire. Taking over is *not* Their purpose.

If there are aliens coming to Earth for rivalry purposes, they would be no match for The Nine. If a territorial Being tried to take over or fight against Them, that Being would be like a mosquito trying to do battle with a flyswatter.

I also know beyond a shadow of a doubt that my past encounters with The Nine have been for the benefit of mankind. They are always loving, highly spiritual and have a great sense of humor. They are always allowing and never controlling.

A year or so after Gene's visit to my home, my Guides told me that I would be asked to go on a book tour with someone. They said that it would be a good idea for me to ask Gene to go along for the interviews as well. He would be able to tell what he saw that night at my home to validate the reality of what was going on.

When I asked him if he would do the interviews with me in the event that the invitation did come to pass, his positive reply was very emphatic. He said, "Yes, I sure will; I know what I saw, and nobody will ever talk me out of that one. This is something that should be told, not only because of you but because of my brother's involvement."

That time did come to pass not too long after my meeting with Gene. In fact, it was the time when Doctor Mack invited me to do his televised book tour.

I called Gene to tell him that this book tour was coming to pass, just as I had been told that it would. I had called to confirm that he was still willing to tell what he saw. He made a total turnaround on me at that time. He told me that he had decided not to do it. He said he had a family and a business to protect. He was afraid to go public with what he saw; he felt that it could wreck his life and business.

When I received the call to do the book tour, I told them that I had a witness that would vouch for the alien presence at my home. After Gene backed out, I had to give them the bad news. After I told them about his concerns, they promised to disguise his voice and face so that he would not be recognized. They wanted this valuable witness. He still refused; I was very disappointed with his reply, but I allowed him free will.

There were other friends that were witness to my encounters that were also afraid. They were concerned that they too could become an abductee. One of those longtime friends, Karen, has totally abandoned our friendship because of these concerns. She dropped out on me even though she had been mesmerized for years with what was going on.

Several of my encounters that took place here on Earth and are not otherwise mentioned in this book involved witnesses of a different kind. Those witnesses were various animals. The animals were terribly frightened by what was happening during each of those encounters.

Lynn is one of my longtime, intuitive friends that are *not* afraid of the encounters. She seems to accept them for what they are and understands that they a part of who I am.

I was still a little shaken after my scary encounter with The Intruder at Lynn's property. I contacted her to tell her that I was thinking about leaving Florida and going back to North Carolina for a while. She convinced me to stay, because she didn't feel it was the right time for me to leave Orlando. I agreed as I valued her intuition and decided to let go of my fear.

I guess the electrifying encounter gave me the jump start that I needed, as I immediately started working on the book again.

Chapter 10
Beamed Up?

I was about to experience the event of my life, and this time there was to be no fear. Lynn was the instrument for this new event; she had assisted in getting me back to Florida, and now she was about to drive me to the right place at just the right time. Over the years, our lives had been intertwined on so many different occasions, and this one was the highlight of my life.

I had been meditating on getting back into the swing of things with my spiritual mission. This meditation seemed to usher in a new set of instructions that came to me with an uplifting feeling. The instructions were for me to go to the Clearwater, Florida, area to spend a couple of days with my friend, Judy.

I called Judy to see what she was up to. She said that my call had come at a perfect time, because she was going to be babysitting at her friend Carmen's home near Clearwater Beach. She invited me to come over for a few days while Carmen was away. I jumped at the chance to be near the beach with Judy. I always enjoyed her company, and I love the balancing energy from the ocean.

I realized I couldn't get to the beach because my car was out of commission again. I told Lynn about my instructions and my dilemma. As luck would have it, she just happened to be going to that area for business at that very same time and offered to drop me off at Carmen's house. This was just another one of those coincidences in my life, or so I thought at the time.

As soon as I got to Carmen's house, I felt an intense spiritual energy in the air; it was almost overwhelming. I don't think I have ever been so peaceful and relaxed as I was that evening. I mentioned the energy to the other girls, but they didn't seem to notice anything out of the norm. They mentioned that there were a lot of crystals in the house and suggested that the crystals might be creating the energy I was feeling. I don't know if they were feeling the same energy that I was, but my hair was practically standing on end the whole evening.

After dinner and chatting with the girls for a while, Carmen had to catch a plane. Judy was extremely tired and wanted to retire early to meditate so we could get an early start the next day. I was enjoying the time to bask in this spiritual energy so that was perfect for me. I chose to relax on the couch to do my reading and meditating.

The energy that I had been feeling quickly took on a new life. I could feel it urging me to recline and get more relaxed. I took my shoes off, and put my feet up on the couch. One minute I was relaxing, and the next second, I could feel my body floating down onto a sandy beach in an upright position. I was quite surprised when I felt my bare feet sink into the soft sand as my body was placed on the beach.

I immediately looked out over the ocean and into the clear, starlit sky. I saw a large number of what appeared to be lights at a great distance. These individual lights seemed circular in shape. They were arranged in a huge circle formation that was rotating in a counterclockwise direction.

I was puzzled by that motion; my mind expected them to rotate in a clockwise direction. I was also puzzled as to why lights of that size would be that far from shore, as they were larger than what you would be seeing at that distance if they were actually lights on a bridge or road. I also sensed that I was not looking in the direction of a road, bridge or a city. This made it more obvious that these lights were not normally located there.

It was also obvious that these lights were not stars; they were too large. They were also moving in unison and held their circle formation while rotating. A powerful, loving and balanced spiritual energy started to build around me as I stood there on the beach. I was totally mesmerized by what was going on and especially mesmerized with this heavenly energy.

All of a sudden, I felt a high frequency, male, God-like presence with me on the beach. By that time, I had realized that I was watching a group of individual spacecrafts out over the ocean. I have to guess but there must have been several dozen of these spacecrafts in the circle; it was an unbelievably huge formation. It was obvious by that time that these lights were individual ships and in no way attached to each other. If I hadn't seen this for myself, I would never have believed that there could be that many spacecrafts here on Earth at one time and presenting themselves all at once.

Everything was happening so fast, from the time my feet landed on the beach and up to this point, there were only split seconds between each event that took place. There was no time to be able to judge what was going on or think about much of anything. I realized later that I had not even questioned how I got to the beach.

As the intensity of the spiritual energy continued to increase around me, I instinctively knew who He and the others in the ships were. I was feeling a soul connection with this God-like presence beside me. The next thought in my head was, "Finally, these are my People. Can I go with You? That thought was read by Them instantly. One of the spacecraft in the circle zipped out of the lower, left side of the rotating group and hovered above my head in a flash. At that very instant, my instinct had been confirmed. My People had finally arrived in Their craft, just as They had earlier promised.

As it hovered above my head, my eyes examined as much of the ship as they could. It was so huge that I could barely see the entire bottom of it at that close range.

The God-like presence was still with me as I stood there on the beach gazing at the beautiful craft above my head. The energy from the craft had such an intense spiritual, yet electrifying, energy that you could have powered an entire city from that energy alone. This intense energy then began to grow and envelope me even more. At that point, this male Entity began to speak to me telepathically; He gave me a very personal message.

After I received my message, I noticed a large, round section in the center of the craft's bottom. It appeared to be used as an opening to the outside. Just then, a wide beam of brilliant, effervescent, white light came out of that center section and touched me on top of the head. This light beam is best described as *Christ White Light* from the feeling it emanated. There was such a power with this beam;

the energy from it felt like God. It was an energy of spiritual love and total perfection.

This white beam and its energy seemed to melt and run through my entire body like liquid. This process started when the beam touched the top of my head. Every cell of my body from head to toe became saturated with the Christ White Light. This Christ White Light had a warm effervescent feeling as it saturated the cells. Once these seemingly millions of cells in my body were saturated, they felt as though they came unglued or separated from each other. They stood in suspension for a second, and then my bare feet lifted from the sand as I quickly floated upward. I lost my conscious thought processes at the point when I was about halfway to the craft.

Some time later, this same process reversed itself, and I was placed back on the beach. As I touched down again, I could feel my bare feet sinking into the deep sand once again. Right after they did, I found myself reclining on the couch and still wide-awake. I was as alert as I was when I first reclined on the couch.

I had a quick flash on the couch of what had happened and quickly relived the entire thing. It felt like the entire experience had been engraved in my soul and brain so that I would not forget anything that had just happened. Trust me, I will never forget the details and the feeling that I had during this experience. A few seconds after reliving my experience, Judy turned a light on in the hallway.

As she came down the hall toward the bathroom, she looked in the living room and saw that I was awake. She told me she had been sleeping, but something had awakened her. She indicated that it was then the wee hours of the morning, just before dawn. I was a little confused at that point and recall looking at her without giving a reply. I must have been gone all night, according to what she had just said.

I had no clue how I got from the couch to the beach or back to the couch again; it all happened so fast. At that time, I was not aware of how something like this was even possible. It just doesn't fit into our earthly reality. I had somewhat of an idea and wondered if it was the same as what had been attempted in the past and been aborted. It definitely seemed to fit in with the science fiction concept of beaming up, but it didn't fit into my reality.

On the first attempt, the process was so slow that I had time to become frightened of it, which caused Them to abort the process. During that attempt, I screamed when the process started because I felt my body's cells start to separate and head toward the window. I was scared out of my wits; I had no idea what was happening at that time. I think the process was much faster the second time, assuming that this was the same process, so that I wouldn't have a chance to be afraid and stop Them again.

This second time around was such a beautiful, spiritual experience. Knowing that I had just spent time with my People from Rising Star was awesome. I can only wish that I had Their power in this earthly body. I guess that wouldn't really be possible; my body would probably explode with the kind of intense energy that They possess. I don't think the human body is constructed for that kind of energy all at once.

This experience left me wanting to know more about my People and to spend more time with Them here on

Earth. I wasn't ready to leave Earth and the people I loved. Most of all, I wasn't about to leave before this mission on Earth was completed.

As I thought about what had happened, I found it quite odd that I didn't tell Judy about the experience. I guess it was a private time for me, and I was also overwhelmed and mesmerized that it had just happened.

As I contemplated this adventure with the God-like Beings, I suddenly understood more of the bigger picture of the so-called beaming event. I realized why I had been told to spend a few days with Judy. I also realized that this incident occurring during my visit with her was more than a coincidence, as I had originally thought. The entire plan had been orchestrated by the God-like Light Beings. I was amazed at Their master planning and timing; it was impeccable, down to the point of timing Lynn's trip to the area. They are master planners for sure.

I am glad I listened to the instructions of these Light Beings instead of ignoring Them, as I had on other occasions. This was and is my best encounter to date, and I am praying for more time with my People while I am on Earth. I now know beyond a shadow of a doubt that my People are real and have been guiding me for a very long number of years. Seeing was believing in this case as well.

All of the bizarre things in my life were finally more believable than ever. Each event over the years has continued to strengthen my belief in what I had originally doubted was real. This event carved that belief in stone for me. If the bizarre experience of meeting my People onboard a spacecraft could be possible, then the other encounters were easily possible. It certainly left nothing to the imagination.

All doubts and skepticism from the past were erased after I spent time with my People.

The speed and beauty of Their craft was remarkable. The craft had gone from being so far out over the ocean to hovering above my head in a split second. I didn't even see it travel the distance. It was still out over the ocean where I first saw it, then it suddenly zipped out of the lower, left side of the circle formation and was above my head instantly. It was either too fast for the naked eye to see or it had dematerialized and then materialized as it arrived. Evidently, my body went through a similar process to get to the beach.

When the craft was hovering, I could feel the intensity of the power that allowed it to function. My entire body sensed the silent power as I stood below it. I wondered if the craft was functioning on some kind of light power, in as much as the craft had such an intense, brilliant, white light.

The round, globe-shaped craft that I had seen in Orlando in 1976 looked nothing like this one. The size, shape, and design of these two crafts were totally different. The Orlando craft was beautiful because of the type of colors and the changes to them as it floated down to Earth. I saw it at a very close range as well, as it was right in front of my car, so there was no guesswork there either. It was spherical in shape and very, very, very tiny in comparison to the new crafts that I encountered at the beach.

The close-up view that I had of the craft at the beach was from the bottom, which was fairly flat and circular. I wasn't able to see the top, so I couldn't see its shape. It was so beautiful and spellbinding because of its detail and functionality—not to mention the God-like energy that emanated from it; that was the best part.

All of the lights on this ship were an intense, brilliant, white, as I said. There were two rows of solid, continuous, one-piece bulbs that went all the way around the craft and glowed with white light. They looked like long, fluorescent tubes shaped into a circle, and as I said, those bulbs ran all the way around the bottom of the ship. There were other, smaller lights that formed individual circles between those two rows of solid bulbs. These individual circles were repeated all the way around the bottom of the craft.

There were a large number of these groups of smaller lights in circular formations pretty close together. Those small lights were either flashing off and on in a way that made them appear to be rotating counterclockwise and in unison, or they could have actually been rotating. I have no way to know that for sure; my logic says that they were actually rotating, and that this had something to do with powering or creating energy for the craft. Otherwise, other than for decorative effect, there would not have been much purpose for them. Once again, I noticed things around these God-like Beings that were operating in the reverse of what I would expect them to be on Earth.

I will venture a guess to the size of this craft. To put it into some perspective, I guesstimate that at *least* six or seven houses, two thousand square feet each, could fit into this one craft, possibly even more than that. The total size of this craft from my vantage point was almost unbelievable, and unimaginable for that matter. I have never seen an object that large on Earth. I am not sure if I would have believed any of this if I had not personally been there to witness and experience it.

I don't remember all that went on during the time that I spent inside the craft, except for a quick flash of seeing myself on a lighted table and a few other details. At a later time, I saw more of the things that occurred when I was inside the craft. I can't remember right now if I had this recall in the regression or by some other means, but it is still very vivid in my memory today. I can't imagine that I would ever forget it; it was so real and unusual, to say the least.

The memory I recalled of my time in this craft started with feeling my physical body inside of it and being able to see the God-like Light Beings there with me. Then in the first room, I saw a large chair in the middle of it. It reminded me of a dentist's chair. I didn't feel the same way about it as I do about the dentist's chair—no dread or fear involved.

The chair didn't seem to have anything to do with me at that time. I just recall walking around the left side of it with two or three Light Beings at my side. We had to walk around the chair to get to another room that was behind it. I saw other items near the walls and around this first room, but I didn't look directly at them. From my vantage point, the center of the room was fairly sparse, except for the chair. I vaguely recall going through the door and into the second room, but I ended up there.

After we walked around the chair, I saw the doorway that we were going to go through. It was like I saw the doorway as we stood in front of it and the next thing I knew I was in another room and my body was laying on a flat table. This table reminded me of a professional tanning bed. There was a brilliant, white light inside this table that made the entire surface of the platform glow. There was no top to the table like a tanning bed would have; from what I could see, it was an open table.

At the foot of the table, there was a flat, lighted piece that came straight up for my feet to rest against. It was slightly taller than my feet were long. I could feel my body lying there on the table and my feet were resting against the lighted piece at the foot of the bed. I had my eyes shut to begin with, and then, I suddenly opened them and looked down toward my feet. When I looked at my feet, I quickly came back into my mental senses, because I was shocked by what I saw. I could see the bones in my feet and legs. I sensed and knew that the rest of my insides were visible as well.

This was when I saw that the entire table was lit with white light; it was an X-ray table, for lack of a better name for it. I now know that my insides were showing through my skin the entire time that I was lying there. It functioned like our X-ray machines; however, this X-ray device had an all-in-one function. The light in the X-ray table stayed on the entire time that they were observing my insides. I do remember seeing the light showing through my eyelids before I opened them. Possibly that is why I opened my eyes to begin with. I wish we had that advanced X-ray table here on Earth. How simple would life be on Earth with an x-ray table that didn't do damage to the physical body and functioned as high-tech as this one did?

The Light Beings evidently realized that I had become alert because I lost that awareness quickly. I do recall that I felt pleased to be with Them at the time that I became alert. I assumed they did something to remedy that situation. I have no more memory of what happened at the time except for walking around the chair and seeing my bones. My next recall was when They bid me goodbye at the door; that part was sad.

During my alert state, I could see two or three, possibly four, very tall, human Light Beings standing directly along the right side of the flat table while I was lying on it. They had a calm, male energy. They wore some kind of lab clothing, scrubs or just plain and simple, free-flowing garments. When I saw Them out of my peripheral vision, They were just standing still and communicating telepathically with each other as They looked at the inside of my body. I was not aware of what They were saying, if anything, at that time.

None of this was disturbing to me because Their energy was calm and peaceful. I knew Them as my People, the people I had known forever. I felt as though I were a part of Them and spiritually connected to Them, so there was no reason to be concerned or afraid. Additionally, it seems that the entire visit was merely so They could introduce Themselves to me and assist me with my health. That's an outlandish thought, but it's the only thing I know about this trip at this point. Meeting Them in person exceeded my wildest imagination!

As you may recall, They had told me ahead of time that They were coming to take me. I just didn't know when or how that would transpire. Back then, I had also told them my concerns about abductions, and Their reply was, "You will be taken; there will be no pain, but the pain you now have will be gone. They were definitely right about that; there was no pain, and the pain I previously had was gone.

I'm always amazed by Their melodic manner of speaking to me and how They always read my thoughts.

As I lay there on the table, I could also see, from my peripheral vision, a white aura of light that surrounded Their entire bodies and garments. These Beings were identical to humans in body form and shape, except that They were extra tall compared to humans on Earth. Their aura was like looking through a haze or mist when I tried to see Their facial features. I don't see auras when I am on Earth, so I thought it was odd that I could see Their auras in that setting. I have many spiritual gifts, but I have never seen a human aura in my life outside of that craft.

I somehow got off the table and back into that first room that was by the entrance. I could feel and sense myself standing there as They bid me goodbye. It was kind of like when you are in the surgery recovery room: you're aware, but you don't remember it with your full senses at the time.

As I stood looking at Them, I could see that They were well over six feet tall and had a sturdy build. Their facial features were fully blocked by this white, glowing aura. I was still trying to see what Their features looked like while we stood at the doorway. I couldn't make them out clearly enough to be able to describe what they looked like.

I was amazed that these Light Beings were so human looking. They also seemed to function as normal bodies except for Their walking; it was almost like gliding or floating. They didn't float off of the floor but moved so gracefully that They almost appeared to be floating.

I hope to be able to gain more information about that visit with Them, if there is more to know. Better yet, another visit would be great. They can take me anytime as long as They bring me back to my immediate family for a while longer, until my final departure from Earth. At that time, I would love to go in that manner.

As you know by now, I have argued with myself about the reality of some of my encounters, always wanting more proof. This proof was over the top. After this experience, I realized that these Beings were the ones that Nasha had told me about, the God-like Light Beings from Rising Star. After that realization, I flashed back to the point in my regression with Doctor Mack where They had come to save my life while I was being born.

At that same time, I recalled another thing that Nasha had told me. She said that my People from Rising Star were coming to take me home. This was the second time I had heard that I was going to be taken; the first was when They told me that same thing. I now wonder if She were referring to my being taken aboard the craft in this same manner. She could also have meant that they were bringing me into a higher consciousness. I have heard that the term *taking you home* also means raising your spiritual consciousness or awareness.

However, after thinking this over, I do think that Her statement referred to Them taking me in Their craft, as opposed to taking me into a higher consciousness. I don't know if Nasha was referring to my People taking me home on this trip or if there will be another trip for me to experience. All I can do now is ask for another trip with Them in Their craft. I found out later that Nasha had been involved with the aborted experience.

I don't know where the craft took me, after picking me up that night. I look forward to a future opportunity to have a new regression or more automatic recall to find more answers to my questions.

One would think that if my People came to take me to my original home that They would not have brought me back. Of course, I guess the obvious reason why would be that I have not finished my mission on Earth yet. The ideal way to leave Earth would be for Them to take me home permanently in this physical body. What I do know beyond a shadow of a doubt is that my People will eventually take me home by the method of Their choosing.

I never would have expected that I would be taken into the spacecraft by these God-like Beings without notice. I had been told to go to that area for a visit, but I just thought it was for a break and a casual visit with the girls. As it turned out, it was the best visit that I have ever had. At this point, I realized that it had to be a surprise to keep me from aborting it once again. I also realized that this particular spacecraft was no longer a UFO; it had become an IFO (Identified flying object).

As a result of my visit from Nasha and my being taken by my People, I was finally able to comprehend the full reality of my new truth and accept all of the encounters that I had lived through up to that point as real.

When They came to get me, They came in full power as opposed to prior visits that were of a lower frequency. This process left no guesswork as to the nature of the experiences I have had my entire life. The things that I had learned as truths through the experiences with the Messengers confirmed my new reality.

In the past, I was often in denial about who I was in relationship to the powerful Messengers from God. I think that is a normal response to something this bizarre. My People truly are one and the same as these God-like Light Beings that I know as The Nine or the Messengers from God.

Now that I think about my past with these Beings, I realize why the idea came to me out of the blue to ask God to show me the mission that I had been put on Earth for. That was way back before I knew anything about the God-like Beings' involvement with my birth. It goes to show you that our higher consciousness always leads us; we just need to pay attention.

After this last experience, I started paying attention to others experiencers. I became curious as to how my experience with my People compared to the encounter that Travis Walton had with a spacecraft. I reviewed the movie about his life, 'Fire in the Sky,' and found that it was nothing like my experience with my People. I found that one difference was that I was taken into a craft by a beam of light and he was knocked down by a beam and then taken by another method. Even though we both ended up in a spacecraft, we got there by a totally different process and we were in the presence of a different alien group, a major difference. He had a harrowing experience in the craft, which was the opposite of mine.

Up to this point in life, I had never heard of anyone in history actually being taken up into a craft in the same manner as I did, except for a brief segment that I saw of a Sci-Fi television show that depicted a person's body breaking apart and moving upward. If I recall it correctly, that body seemed to go through a tubular apparatus of some kind. I didn't watch the entire movie or show as I have never been interested in Sci-Fi stories.

I now know beyond a shadow of a doubt that I have not completed my mission on Earth just yet, but I am on the way to finishing this God-given mission. I am truly grateful for my highly spiritual experiences and the fact that I have never experienced anything like Travis did.

All was well and ended well after my beautiful trip aboard the spacecraft with my People…until next time.

Chapter 11
The Plot Thickens

The plot thickens, as they say. Just when I thought I had been taught everything that the God-like Messengers had to teach me, They surprised me again. I kept thinking that They were ready for me to wrap up the text for the book, and then I found that I did not have all of the information I was to disseminate. Additional information may still keep coming, but I have definitely received a large number of answers to the mysteries of the ages, enough to create an entirely new reality for the public—for those who are willing to read with an open mind. Every day seems to be a new learning experience for me; however, at that point, I soon learned that the most spiritually enlightening experience was just ahead of me.

I usually think outside the box, but my lack of ego would never have allowed me to create a scenario in my mind where I would be taken up into a craft on a beam with a group of God-like Messengers and meet my People from another planet.

My next experience was even more bizarre, and due to my teachings from church, I would never have imagined such a thing. Although, this new information makes a lot more sense than what I had learned in church.

A number of years after being taken up and into the craft of my People, I received a shocking, spiritual revelation that was created for me by the Messengers. At the time that this information came to me, I was relaxing on my patio to watch the clouds roll by. All of a sudden, a heavenly realm opened and a complex and detailed revelation was given to me by the Messengers. It was a complex message that rang true. I was mesmerized by the new information that I had been shown. I quickly went to get my trusty tape recorder to record the entire event.

In this revelation, the Messengers told me that I had *not* been beamed up as I originally thought. They said that the beaming up process is science fiction, and in reality, it is only fiction, as there is no such thing. They went on to say, "What actually happened the night that you were taken into the craft is not considered a beaming up process. It was the Ascension process. You actually Ascended, just as Jesus did. "

They went on to say, "The Biblical Rapture will take place in the future. When it does transpire, the Ascension process will take place again for a large number of people. Those people will also Ascend, just as Jesus did." They also said, "This is what the Rapture process is." I was totally shocked, but I knew in my heart it was true. Who would imagine that others and I would actually Ascend in the way that Jesus did?

My mission on Earth has become clearer. Now that I know about my origin and have the Ascension and rapture knowledge as well as the answers, to the mysteries of the ages, I have a better understanding of why I have to be the spokesperson for these nine Messengers from God. I, indeed, must disseminate this information. What a great mission to be chosen for. I knew that They had chosen me for a mission, but I didn't have a clue as to how important this mission would be for myself and humanity in general.

I also see that the purpose for my own Ascension was multifaceted. As far as the public goes, it was for allowing the world to know that anyone can Ascend. The chosen ones like me, and there are many of us on Earth, have the God-given right to Ascend during the Rapture or at any given second. There will be many new chosen people on Earth in the future as well as the ones currently existing. We all have the ability to create what we want in our lives, and being a chosen one is not off limits.

Of course, Jesus was a chosen person and the Son of God. He was here on Earth for His own mission. I always lived my life with the intention of being the best Christian and person I could be, even before I realized I was here for a specific mission. I always felt as though I had known Jesus forever as a close friend and have seen Him in visions many time during meditation. I am not sure why I felt as though I knew Him; however, I do not think of myself as an equal to Him. According to the Bible, Jesus manifested material things and performed many other kinds of miracles, as well as being a great teacher and prophet. At this stage of spiritual evolution, I could never come close to doing anything He did on Earth. Therefore, I want to make it clear that I am not implying that I am an equal to Him or that I can do any of those things that He did here. He did so much more than Ascend.

The only comparison I am making is that we both Ascended in the same manner, according to the Messengers from God. Jesus knew who He was. A lot of us, in fact most of us, do not know who we really are or what our purpose on Earth is.

This new information about Ascension and the Rapture are two more of the secrets to the mysteries of the ages. Again, just more pieces of the puzzle that help to create the new reality that I now know beyond a shadow of a doubt is true. These new facts will make us a little more up-to-date on what is real and what is possible.

I feel that these truths have been hidden from us. It is time that the facts were given to the people on Earth so they can live their lives in their own true reality, as opposed to living them by someone else's instructions and rules. Each person will find his or her own truth with these new guiding factors of ultimate truth. We are all in total control of our destinies and our lives. We have the power to create the lives we want with the God-given tools that we were born with.

We don't need a go-between to intervene for us with God; we can communicate with God ourselves because of the direct connection we have always had with our Creator.

All of this goes to show you that there is no need for us to be in fear of anything about life and death. We need to think outside the box; contemplate what you have read in this chapter and book to take back your own power and live life to the fullest. No fears, no regrets. Find your mission and move on with a light heart and laughter. Send love to the world and to all you meet. You are in total control of your destiny and your life. Create the life you want with the tools that you were born with; they are God-given.

We have been programmed with teachings about God, life, death, et cetera. The problem is that certain pertinent information has been left out of the equation. The result for me was that my church education didn't add up. The new reality that I have gained does not paint the same picture that my past Christian teachings did. Of course, those teachings were handed down to those teachers at the time, and they bought the truth that they were handed then.

Here is a perfect example of how I was programmed: I thought I had been beamed up at the time I met my People, because I had heard about Scotty being beamed up for years. His body was depicted as being broken up in a similar manner to how my body felt when my cells came apart before Ascending. I often used the term, *beamed up*, as a fact or a truth. I accepted it as fact just as I had accepted what I had been taught in church and by religious leaders. Even though my gut feeling was that something didn't add up, there were no answers available for me to prove otherwise at that time.

For the most part, we only know what we are taught. It is up to us to use our gut feelings to discern truth from fiction. I know I can't be the only one that felt something wasn't right about some of the Biblical teachings and the way that they were interpreted or taught.

When I asked questions in Sunday School class, there were no real answers. The reply was always something like "These are things that we are not supposed to know." This type of teaching has stopped many of us from realizing our full potential and that we are more than physical bodies that live, die, and wait in a grave until Jesus comes back to get us from them. I now know beyond a shadow of a doubt that not everything I had been taught in church was accurate.

When I received the new information about Ascension and the Rapture, my gut feeling was, "Aha! That feels right and it certainly makes a lot of sense compared to my prior teachings from people on Earth." To me, this was a huge piece of the puzzle, and at this point, I feel that the picture is now complete for me.

Over the years, I have met many people in meditation groups who say they have been working hard to gain their own soul evolutions and to increase their spiritual awareness through a number of different methods. Their hopes were to enable themselves to bodily Ascend during one of their meditations.

They were somewhat accurate in their thinking, according to what I have learned from the Messengers. However, what has come to me about it is that these people with a higher spiritual evolution are actually raising their consciousness to prepare or make themselves eligible to Ascend during the future Rapture experience that I have spoken of rather than Ascending at any given moment during meditation because of their spiritual level alone. They could be correct in their thinking as well. I am not ruling out the possibility of a monk like person actually Ascending without the Rapture. They could also be taken into a craft by the Ascension process due to their mission or level of consciousness, just as I was. At this point, I have learned that just about anything is possible.

Now that I know beyond a shadow of a doubt that I actually Ascended, my mind-set about my mission has changed a bit. I now see it as much larger and more important than what I had originally thought. I understand that I Ascended for the purpose of showing others that they too can achieve this, in addition to being able to meet my People and understand more about my mission. The experiences and encounters that seemed like a personal and private matter are no longer private.

In the past, I hid a lot of my experiences from people that were close to me, because I felt as though these experiences were far too personal to share and in some cases, for fear of being judged and ostracized.

This is no longer about me and personal experiences; it is about preparing the public for their future by giving them the facts and bringing them back to the basics, basics that we were never privileged with in the past. With all of this new information, people will have more faith in God, as well as life in general, and realize who they really are. They will know that they also came here for a purpose, and they, too, will be able to fulfill their destiny. With that said, I will have to forget my personal privacy concerns and move forward with my eyes shut.

Sometimes, all of this still feels like a dream to me, but I realize that I have been awakened, and that I have been wide-awake through all of my encounters, at least the encounters that I know and write about!

I try to never allow this work to be like work. I try to keep a sense of humor, as do The Messengers, and The Ascended Masters. While sitting at the computer and writing one day, contemplating all of the reasons for my Ascension, a note of humor popped in. I thought to myself that it was interesting that a male Ascended, and now, a female has

Ascended. I guess God is an equal opportunity boss, with no discrimination for this chosen assignment.

All humor aside, I now know beyond a shadow of a doubt that I have still not completed my mission on Earth, but I am working hard to complete it.

It is quite bizarre for me to realize that I am the first modern-day-person to report their Ascension. I now realize that my Ascension was a *Close Encounter of The Nine Kind*.

With this encounter, and all of the other well kept secrets I have learned that are answers to the mysteries of the ages, I have gained a new reality that I am happy to share with the world.

Chapter 12
Reverse Polarity

I have always understood that the left side of the body is supposed to be the receiving side when spiritual Guides are imparting information to us. The information from the spiritual Being is transmitted and received through the aura of the human body.

I have found this to be different when my People come to me. When They want to impart information to me, They appear on my right side and then transmit that information to me from Their energy. This is another thing that makes me feel as though Their polarity is in the reverse of ours.

This has been the case, not only on the night of the delayed energy transfer, but during every other visit with Them as well. Everything about the God-like Beings seems to operate counterclockwise, the opposite of the way we function.

After I have been with Them and return to my earthly realm, I notice that things on Earth seem to be functioning in reverse. Everything seems as though it is being done backwards, and it causes me to feel disoriented. This feeling often lasts for days after I have been with Them; it is maddening. Other times, it gradually leaves me sooner.

Now that I think about this, I have had several bouts of vertigo. I wonder if that imbalance might be caused by going out of the earthly energy flow and into a reverse energy flow during my encounters and visits. When I come back to Earth and leave Their energy flow, it seems to cause some disruption in my balance. I don't know a medical term for this; it is just a wild thought. However, it may not mean anything at all. I would like to check into this theory a little more thoroughly.

These Light Beings seem to be in the natural flow of God's energy. When I am with Them, everything feels so balanced. When I'm back in the earthly space, the energy feels unnatural. Could Earth be messing up the flow of energy in the Universe? If we are, in fact, functioning in the reverse of other planets, we may be hampering their progress. If so, how did Earth end up operating in the reverse of other planets?

Something about Earth definitely feels as though things are not quite right or out of sync with the rest of the Universe. I have often felt this when I return from other dimensions that I temporarily exist in. I feel that the entire Universe needs to be in sync and flowing in unison to progress and evolve. If we are the only planet functioning in a clockwise motion, could this be causing the negative energy here since everything is energy? I have a strong, gut feeling that someday, we will learn that the Earth is functioning in reverse, maybe even rotating in reverse.

My body functions better when I spend more time with my People. At those times, I feel that I am in the flow of nature. Their energy is so balanced, therefore creating balance within me. If Their loving, positive energy could be felt on Earth at all times, it would be a heavenly place to live.

As I have said previously, when I return to Earth, I feel a lot of negativity. I feel that it will take a lot of doing, but that can be changed to positive energy. If we all send love to Earth, the Universe, and all we meet on a regular basis, it will change the energy around us, and that energy also extends out to the entire Universe. Every little bit helps; just like going green, every little bit that we contribute to the Earth and the Universe is helpful.

Chapter 13
Restructuring

My friend Glenn from Georgia had just purchased a new home and invited me to come for a visit. I had been instructed to give a lecture in Atlanta, and his home was on the way. The timing worked out perfectly, so I decided to take him up on his offer.

I accepted the invitation without thinking about all of the chemical smells that linger in a new home. This turned out to be a crucial error on my part, as I am very sensitive to chemicals and anything that has a smell.

I arrived at Glenn's house late in the afternoon. The evening became a little chilly, so he decided to light the wood-burning fireplace. I realized that my sensitivity to smoke might make me sick. It was almost time to retire, so instead of saying anything, I just hoped that I wouldn't smell the smoke in the upstairs guest room. I didn't want to be rude by telling him about my sensitivity to it, so I went off to bed.

Unfortunately, the smoke did drift to the upper levels of the house. I was awakened in the night because I was violently ill. I spent the next two days in bed with terrible nausea and felt like I was going to die.

I got worried as the second evening approached, and I was still violently ill. I was booked in Atlanta the night after that. I was desperate, so I prayed about it and talked to the

Messengers about my problem, as They had instructed me to do the lecture. I telepathically told Them that They were going to have to create a miracle for me if I was going to be able to do the lecture.

Just about the time I finished my request to Them, I felt an object placed over my head. It was shaped like a large, round bubble. It was clear and felt like a plastic helmet that only touched my neck area. I could see through it while my head was encased. I felt an intense energy inside the bubble that increased. I didn't remember anything after that. I awoke the next morning totally refreshed; it was as if I had never been sick. I had never heard of a healing taking place like this, but the Messengers have many unique tools for healing and diagnosing health that we do not have on Earth. Each one that I have seen and have had used on my body has been a major surprise to me.

Believe me; I have never been more grateful for a healing. It was too bad that I didn't ask for healing earlier, but I was so ill that I wasn't thinking clearly. Better yet, I should have asked if I should spend time at Glenn's house before I went there. They are really big on allowing me free will. They assign me a mission, and my brain takes over from there. I need to remember to start asking for additional guidance instead of using so much brainpower. However, I realize that They have more to do than babysit me, but I knew that this lecture was very important to both of us.

There have been numerous healings to my body from the Light Beings throughout my life. This is just one of the many blessings that They have given me.

As I mentioned earlier, I am quite sure that the Light Beings have me monitored. They show up when I am in need of physical healing or ask Them for assistance. In one instance, these Beings protected me from danger and then removed the intense fear I was unable to let go of. They did this by performing a minor restructuring process on my solar plexus area. That visit at Glenn's home is a perfect example of the Light Beings knowing my location as well as when I need help.

My healings have come to me in so many different ways. Most have been through energy transfers to my body. However, I never rule anything out for the future due to the number of variations that I have experienced so far.

I was born with a body that seems to be normal most of the time, but I inherited genes that have a few problems. I have required a number of healings due to deficiencies in my body, as well as from being exposed to so many toxins. I also burn the candle at both ends, which doesn't help much.

Medical doctors have been somewhat helpful, but the long-lasting healing nearly always comes from the energies of the Light Beings. I share my Cousin, Tim's, experience in that he has noticed that doctors can always tell him what he doesn't have.

To maintain a healthy body, the Light Beings often tell me which supplements or foods I need for better health.

There are far too many healings They have done for me to detail each one, but another interesting one that I recall occurred while I was reclining against a huge pile of pillows on my waterbed. At the time this occurred, I was having irregular heartbeats, so I decided to lay down on the waterbed until my heart calmed down. As soon as I reclined against the pillows, I felt something pressing against my back in the heart area. It felt just like the barrel of a gun. I thought that was strange, because I was lying against all of these pillows. How could I feel something like that while lying against the soft pillows!

Just then, a powerful energy transferred to me through this hard instrument that corrected the heart problem. At first, I was really scared; the intense energy kept flowing through my body for what seemed like a several minutes. My first thought was that I was being electrocuted by the waterbed. I looked over at the electrical outlet and saw that the bed was unplugged. At that point, I realized that I had just had another intervention.

I reported this incident to Doctor Mack to get his take on the matter. He remarked that several of his subjects had also had similar experiences.

A few years prior to that healing, while living in Orlando, I had another unusual healing that was more bizarre than the others. I had been experiencing problems in my upper abdominal area. The healing began just as I got into bed and relaxed. I felt the upper part of my body lying solidly against the sheets when all of a sudden, I felt an intense spiritual energy in the room and around my body. Then, the lower part of my body, from the upper abdomen down, started sliding downward on the sheets. I could actually feel my body sliding; I was essentially separated at the middle. At that point, it felt as though something was going on inside my body.

After this procedure was finished, I noticed that I no longer had the pains I had previously experienced. Unfortunately, I have begun to experience problems in this area again in recent years. I hope it is not from something that I have created through diet or some other means, but I am looking forward to a healing once again.

Another unusual incident occurred in April, 2006. I had been ill due to a number of nutritional deficiencies. My heart and lungs had become an issue for me. It was mostly due to the fact that I was overworked and wasn't eating properly. I also had not been taking enough time to balance my physical and spiritual body. At that time, I was unable to sleep unless I sat straight up in a chair. After a few nights of that, I awoke to something pressing against the upper rib cage through my back. Again, I thought that was impossible, because my back was against a soft, padded chair. I quickly realized what was happening as I flashed back to the time of the healing on the waterbed.

During this incident, I was wide-awake because of the intensity of the energy transfer that was taking place. At first, I felt two oval-shaped, cushioned, objects pressing on each side of my upper back. They felt like they were about three inches wide and reminded me of the larger-sized, stereo headphones that are cushioned.

A very strong energy radiated from the center of these objects and penetrated my entire chest cavity. It became almost unbearable due to the intensity of the energy and the pressure that was being forced against my back. I realized what was happening, so I yelled at Them to stop hurting me. I was ignored. About that time, my chest felt like it was expanding; it became huge and felt hollow. It was as if I had a large balloon in my chest that had caused it to expand. The pain and the energy stopped after the expansion completed, and then it deflated. I was breathing freely again, and my lungs felt normal after the procedure.

At that point, I felt really stupid. I had reprimanded Them for helping me with a crisis. I guess They understand that the human brain cannot comprehend or act as fast as They can. Nobody on Earth could possibly keep up with these Light Beings; They can act faster than the brain can comprehend.

A few months later, I was having chest discomfort before falling asleep. Again, I asked for healing so that I could be totally well, as I needed to get back to work on my book. After I fell asleep, I awoke with a pain in my chest. This pain was for a different reason. I felt something moving through the blood vessels in my chest. The vessels felt huge, and I could feel a tool that pulsed as it moved through them. It felt pointed and sharp as it moved; it was very painful. It felt like a mini jackhammer as it made its way through the vessels. I could see inside my body with my mind's eye and saw exactly what was happening. After these last two procedures, I was much healthier.

On another occasion, I recall asking for healing, this time for a different issue. They quickly obliged with two days of intense energy applied to my body to get rid of the problem.

When I was younger, I cautiously dealt with these kinds of events but didn't share them. Most of us are programmed by the rule setters of our Earth to be in fear of this kind of thing. You know the routine: it might be something evil! I often wonder why people never have the thought that it might actually be God in action instead.

As the years moved on, I shared my experiences even less, because I had become aware of my alien encounters. I was pretty sure that I would have been considered a nut at that point. I felt like I would be judged for living a normal life—normal to me, anyway.

That was how I lived until I learned that all of these experiences are a part of spiritual growth. That was helpful for me to know. It was also helpful that others started reporting their alien encounters. I didn't feel so alone then, even though their encounters were nothing like mine. At least they were dealing with aliens that come to Earth in spacecraft, which made me feel less like of a kook. Their events allowed me to come out of the closet with my life a little bit more. After all, the public basically know about aliens in general but I have never heard one account that is even similar to my life's story with The Nine.

As time went on, I learned a lot more about the soul body. I learned that all humans possess both physical and spiritual, or soul, bodies. I had my picture taken by the Kirlian photography method, which is a camera that photographs your aura. I was able to see my physical and soul body in the photograph. I saw other photographs on display there and noticed that each and every soul body looked different.

While we are living, we need to balance these two bodies. As I understand it, we can help raise the vibrational frequency level of our spiritual and physical bodies while incarnated. I feel like this will assist us in going to a higher level when we pass from this plane of existence, merely due to the fact that like attracts like.

Our soul body has been and always will be the same original soul that we were in the beginning of time. That soul will have a new physical body for each incarnation. It is more in depth than that, but I am not an expert on the terminology of the entire process. I now know beyond a shadow of a doubt that we are here for the learning process and to evolve spiritually.

Spiritual growth is a pleasant experience. We should all accept it and enjoy life and the ability to be able to be exposed to such a higher power while in a physical body. We live in a physically minded planet, which makes it harder to evolve spiritually. Sometimes, the brain is too much in control, which causes the spiritual body to function less in our lives. That is the soul body battling the brain. The brain wants to win.

You can manifest a higher consciousness just by desiring it. The more emotion you put into the desire, the more you will receive into your consciousness. You can also manifest material things in your life with the same process. Again, the amount of desire and emotion that you put into manifesting any one thing that you want in your life, the more you will receive. We all have that power.

It seems that our soul growth in this day and age has been pushed to the side for the sake of living more in the physical and material realm. With the age of technology, we are also more exposed to violence and negativity, which is tainting our souls. All of these things are a deterrent to our spiritual growth.

My main priority is to manifest a higher level of consciousness, as opposed to manifesting material things. It is very easy to get out of balance when manifesting the material things in our lives becomes the main focus. Once you focus on raising your consciousness, the rest will fall into place. Just the other day, I was reflecting on how lucky I have been to be guided to things that have recently worked out well financially for me. At that time, I received a telepathic message, "When you work for God, God works for you." I rest my case.

The tools that I have had available for raising my consciousness, or soul's spiritual level are, meditation, spiritual studies, and spiritual intervention. I have been fortunate to have been led to the spiritual studies that I needed for the raising of my consciousness as well. This has been done through all of my guides: The Nine and the Ascended Masters.

These Guides have also been performing restructuring on my physical body since 1985, as I mentioned earlier in the book. This has been another great tool that raises my spiritual awareness. Restructuring is a process that changes the cells of my body in order for them to resonate at a vibrational frequency that is similar to Theirs. In this process, an energy is transferred to my body. This in turn raises the consciousness of my soul body to make it more spiritually evolved.

When the process is implemented, it is extremely intense and powerful. It feels like electricity penetrates every cell of my body at once. It is very tingly, and I can feel each cell being electrified, but it doesn't actually hurt. It is similar to the Ascension process in the way it feels, yet stronger, and a little different.

This process has always taken place when I am awake, as far as I know, anyway. It has taken place at various locations on Earth. Often times, it occurs when They instruct me to go to a specific location.

In the past, I have been told by several friends that a change in my frequency level has been noticeable. They have remarked that my energy is very calming and healing. This same enhanced energy has also given me an ability to gain answers to the unknown just by thinking a question at a time when I am in spiritual balance.

It is also my understanding that when the higher, spiritual-level energies are transferred to the physical and soul body, they can create a healing, or rebalancing, as well as raising one's consciousness. A total healing can come from them, but that depends on the intensity of the energy that is being transferred at the time. I have been told that the physical body would not be able to tolerate the full extent of energy that could actually be transferred to one's body.

Another variation of energy transfer is the process that Van told me about. He told me that one of my parallel lives had never incarnated in a body and was still in a divine state. He said It had been merging with my consciousness in my current, physical body. That is not exactly the same process, but for generalities, it is similar. In reality the merging process that Van spoke of is also a restructuring process, however, there is an energy transfer that takes place during that process. I am looking forward to seeing the end result of this process and what my next mission will be after the merging is complete.

To make contact with a higher source in meditation, we must consciously raise our vibration or frequency level. It is only a temporary change in frequency under those conditions. If it is done often enough, that alone would help to raise one's frequency more quickly and permanently. You can retain some of that energy each time.

At the time when I met Lee Harris, I felt the intensity of the energy, but that was an energy sharing and not a transfer. That energy was powerful because we are Soul Mates, according to Nasha. We both felt the intensity of the energy; it was way out of the norm, but it wouldn't be comparable to the intensity of the restructuring process.

In my teachings, I have learned that everything is energy, even God. Everything functions at a specific vibrational frequency. Anything can become more solid or less solid to the naked eye in a split second. There are various dimensions all around us that we do not see, because they operate at a different frequency than we do.

Anyone can be functioning in another dimension, another so-called time, or in both in a split second. It can be done by changing the vibrational frequency at will, or with the use of equipment, such as time travel devices.

By focusing on raising our vibrational frequency and our consciousness or spiritual levels, we will be able to connect with God's energy and other Enlightened Beings more easily. Those humans with pure intent can also connect with Beings from another planet that are of a higher vibrational level.

The God-like Beings use Their abilities to change Their frequency at will. With these frequency changes, Their physical bodies and Their spacecraft can appear or disappear instantly. I have witnessed Them and Their crafts change solidity right before my eyes. By using this same process, They can also go through walls or cause our bodies to do the same.

Many times, I have been spaced out as I walked through the house only to find myself functioning in a so-called past or future life. However, there is no such thing as time. Everything past, present, and future are all going on at the same time. So in essence, I drifted into one of those timeless zones, participated, and later came right back into my body in our current time and space. When we leave this physical body and go into another dimension, we will always come back to our body, assuming that we have not permanently left it during the so-called death event. Our silver cord, a term used for an invisible cord, so to speak, keeps our soul connected to the physical body while we are alive.

I have been told by a Guide that I also have a parallel life that is incarnated at this time and is living in the United States right now. My friend Cindy has also seen one of her parallel lives who is currently living on Earth in a foreign country.

I now know beyond a shadow of a doubt that we are living many lifetimes in many different dimensions. As it turns out, we are living all of these lives at once. Now I realize why I'm so tired!

Chapter 14
X-Ray Vision

Back in my early days of my mission, I experienced X-ray vision on two different occasions. Amazingly enough, I was able to see through solid objects both times.

I had been putting a lot of emotion and desire into manifesting more free time to spend on spiritual studies and meditation. I was obsessed about raising my spiritual awareness. I felt that the only way I could have full-time hours for this pursuit would be to quit working. To quit working, I would have to manifest more money. Instead of putting the emotion into the financial end of things, I focused on not having to work to free up my time.

This was around the time that Sue and I witnessed the first UFO. After seeing that UFO, I became like Richard Dreyfuss in the movie *Close Encounters of the Third Kind*. The only difference between him and me was that I didn't create huge mounds out of everything in sight, but I definitely had an obsession going on. That movie was in 1977, and I saw the first UFO in 1976.

I soon learned that thoughts can become things. The good news was that I found out I was pretty good at manifesting. The bad news was that I didn't realize that to manifest something in a desirable manner, you have to be very specific with the details.

My desire was focused on free time to do spiritual study, et cetera, instead of actually focusing on manifesting the money that I would need to quit work. As a result, I manifested an auto accident for myself. I was not able to work for quite some time. I had to be hospitalized and put into traction for a while.

During my hospital stay, the nurses periodically came in to give me a nerve pill. I took a couple of pills during the first day of my hospitalization. After that, I didn't take any more. I got rid of the rest of the pills when the nurses weren't looking.

I was afraid of getting addicted to these pills. I had never been a pill taker of any kind; in fact, when I did have to take one, I usually had a bad reaction to it, so I just did my best to stay away from pills altogether.

The doctor wanted me to be sedated, silent, and in a darkened room while I was in traction. I had to wear a thick, black mask that I couldn't see through to block the bright lights of the hallway when the door to my room was opened.

Near the end of my week in traction, I had a weird experience that was new to me. The nurses had kept the door to my room closed for silence. I was sleeping when someone suddenly opened my door without knocking. I saw the nurse standing in the doorway and the hall lights blaring. She had come to give me my meds. I realized that I still had the mask on as I tried to open my eyes. The strange part was that I saw her and the lights before I removed my mask. I saw her as clearly as if I had no mask on at all. It was definitely X-ray vision. I tried to see through the mask in bright sunlight, and I couldn't see a thing.

After I got home, I kept thinking about what had happened, and I was still amazed that it did. A short time later, I received a phone call from a family member; she was calling to say that they were coming to visit for a week or so. Included in this visit were several children. I was a little concerned about them coming, because I had just gotten home from that long period of silence and darkness. Every little thing seemed to be getting on my nerves because of the immediate change in my environment.

I wanted to see my family, so I was happy that they were coming to visit, even though I was still going to have to stay in traction most of the time. They didn't stay as long as planned, because my body was not able to cope with all of the sudden changes.

After my family left, I was more upset, because they had made the effort to come visit, and I really wanted to visit with them. I knew they would not be having another vacation anytime soon. I felt guilty about not being able to visit with them. All the stress was adding to my condition and left me with no choice but to get something for this nervous condition.

I had not been taking the medicine in the hospital that the doctor gave me, but I felt it was time. I would need to take it to cope with all that was going on as well as my physical problems. I called the doctor to explain and asked if I could get the prescription that they had given me in the hospital.

The pharmacy called and said that the doctor had called and they would bring my prescription over in an hour or so. I was finally able to relax a little knowing that I was going to get the meds to deal with the situation.

I got back in my traction harness and decided to relax and pray for a healing to get me out of my misery. Just as I put my mask back on and relaxed, I saw through the ceiling and was looking at the clouds. I was so surprised by this event that I jerked the mask off. When I took it off, I saw my bedroom again with the ceiling intact. This was prior to taking any medication.

That was such a shocker that I started praying really hard for Jesus to help me with my situation. Just then, there was a loud pop. This sound came from the very dead center of my ceiling. I felt an intense energy coming into the room, and I was suddenly healed of the disturbing feelings that I was having.

Shortly after the healing, the doorbell rang, so I got up to pay the delivery person for the meds. As I got up, I realized that I no longer had a nervous problem. I immediately destroyed the bottle of pills that they had delivered and never needed any medication after this event. I got back into my traction without a nervous condition and continued to heal the natural way. I also had the time to meditate a lot more and do some spiritual studies as I had wanted to do in the first place.

It was obvious to me at that time that I had not mastered this manifesting thing; I had taken the difficult route instead. However, I did ultimately achieve the manifestation in a much larger way. It came about several years later in my mission, but only after I had decided that it was time to take better care of myself. That decision to take care of myself without depending on Them, came about after I started thinking about the world's mess that They were concerned with.

I wanted to achieve my financial goal of creating a more self-sufficient way of life, in order to continue my mission with the Messengers and be able to take care of my health. Once I had made this decision, everything fell into place. Through contemplation and meditation, my intuition guided me to create a unique business model that proved to be very successful. Through that venture I was able to continue my mission, and I got that house just as promised; in fact, I bought two houses, one each in two different states. The only thing that held me up from getting that house sooner was me.

As a result of the processes I have undergone with the Messengers, I was not only able to improve my finances with the new venture, but I now have the ability to visualize inventions and designs for the future on a regular basis. I have already created a few of them and plan to create more in the future. Now, if I can just remember to take the time for nutrition and the spiritual balance necessary for a healthy life, I will be just fine.

Chapter 15
Living Between Worlds and Near-Death Experience

I have had quite a busy life so far. It seems as though this lifetime has been mostly about learning what the reality of life is. As a result of that learning, I now know beyond a shadow of a doubt that Earth is not the only inhabited area of God's Universe. There are many life-forms existing out there.

The events of my life may seem bizarre and impossible to those living with a socially conscious mind-set; I should know because I used to be one of them. To others, these events may seem more like science fiction than reality. However, I have discovered through all of them that there is truth in this new *real reality*, and that truth always resonates with my soul.

Those who don't believe in this real reality cause a lot of stress in their lives by having a constant, subconscious fear of death. Some are always trying to beat the clock before their time runs out. By being open-minded and having more faith, they will eventually realize that life goes on forever and that there is no such thing as death to fear. Today is the first day of the rest of their lives, and they have forever to get things done.

After reading this book, there will be many who have an open mind and open heart who will be empowered by the information in it. It will allow them to discover their own truths by thinking outside the box. My experiences and teachings have definitely opened my eyes to this new reality.

In this lifetime, I have experienced what it's like to be born, live, and die, as well as what it's like living on the other side, after so-called death. I'm obviously living a life on Earth, but at times, I'm also living somewhere between Earth and other worlds of existence, as well as in other worlds of existence.

In 1970, I experienced what it's like to die through a near-death experience (NDE). Since it was such a powerful spiritual experience, I have kept it fairly private until now.

After this experience, I read a lot of metaphysical books to learn more about what had actually happened to me. I learned that NDEs are very real and have been experienced by many. In a true near-death episode, a person actually dies. His or her soul or spirit body leaves the physical body to die. Then sometime later, it returns to the physical body and resumes living.

My NDE occurred while I was sitting in the car at a drive-in theater with my husband, Robert. As a funeral scene took place, I watched the hearse drive down a bumpy road with the casket inside. I suddenly left my body and went into the casket. I could feel each bump on the road as I lay on the satin lining of it.

When I found myself there, my first thought was, "Wow, I'm dead! This is neat." I was glad I was dead, because I had such a calm, spiritual feeling of being at one with God. Then I realized that I no longer had the aches and pains I had been experiencing for a couple of years due to severe anemia.

It was strange to be void of pain or other bodily sensations yet still able to feel the satin against my skin.

My next thought was, "It doesn't hurt to die." I felt great; there was no hot and no cold, and the temperature was neutral. I found it extremely comfortable to be dead. The death process was so effortless; one minute, I was alive, and the next second, I was dead.

After a period of time in the casket, I left that peaceful, quiet environment and abruptly slammed back into my physical body with a jolt. For a split second, I was surprised at finding myself back in the car. The next thing I noticed was the loud, noisy, theater speakers. This horrible noise was a shock to my entire being after coming back from such a peaceful silence. I came back into my physical body in a very harsh manner.

My attention was quickly diverted to Robert, who sat there crying. He was not the kind of person to let me see him be emotional; of course, he wasn't expecting me to see him crying, either.

I asked him what was wrong, because at that moment, I had no memory of what had happened to me. He said he thought I was dead. He said my eyes had been wide open and frozen in place. He had waved his hand in front of my eyes, I didn't blink, and he couldn't detect a breath. He had been afraid to touch me for fear I would fall over. I was puzzled and didn't know why he'd thought I was dead. It was strange that I could have forgotten that quickly about being in the casket.

We went right back to watching the movie and didn't discuss the incident again that evening. The next day as I was walking through the house, I flashed back on the entire event. I had a total recall of what had happened the night before. Each and every detail of my NDE had been regained and I was again puzzled by the fact that that I could have forgotten that I had apparently deceased.

Robert walked in the house just after I had the flashback. I was so excited about what I recalled and wanted to share the details of my NDE with him. I started to tell him what had actually occurred, but he didn't want to hear it. He turned as white as a ghost at the first mention of it. He said he didn't want to talk about it. He turned around and walked out the front door and didn't come back for hours. I never brought the subject up to him again.

I know it sounds like I must have been on drugs at the time of the NDE. I had not taken any drugs or medication whatsoever, not even an aspirin. However, I did have that anemia problem. The anemia was immediately cured by the NDE; however, it did come back a few years later.

I eventually got a divorce from Robert, but we still remain friends. During the divorce proceedings, he told me he was afraid of me. He was concerned about all of the supernatural events happening in my life and he didn't know a thing about my encounters with The Nine. He may never speak to me again after he hears those details because he was and is afraid of what he doesn't understand. He actually knew very little about my supernatural life at all except for what he experienced with me at various times. Back then I didn't share those kinds of things with anyone. What he couldn't understand was how I could always know where he was at a given time and what he was doing; this was what spooked him more than anything. Most of all, he didn't understand what he had witnessed at the drive-in theater: my coming back from the dead.

He spent his school years in a religious school environment. He didn't understand my life, because he had been programmed in the same manner that I had been as a child. He went into the military and lost faith in everything after seeing friends die. I don't think he even believed in God then. He seemed to have adopted the idea that all of his religious teachings had been a lie due to his confusion on these matters. He witnessed and experienced one thing and was taught another. I rest my case!

Now that he is older, he isn't afraid to talk about my gift of intuition; in the past, he avoided any conversation about anything New Age or metaphysical. He jokes about me being psychic almost every time we speak. He likes to give me a hard time about it by using the term *psycho* instead of *psychic,* but he does it in jest. The subject usually comes up because when I speak to him, I still know things about him or his family that I have no way of knowing.

Our supernatural experiences often get swept under the rug out of fear and lack of knowledge about these very natural matters. Knowledge is the key. The teachings in this book will help a lot of people find that key.

There will be more new knowledge to come from the Messengers. One very interesting fact that I have already been informed about, is the process that is already in action to a small degree, small compared to our future ability to utilize it on an everyday basis. At that time there will be an awakening for everyone and a rude awakening for some who choose to deceive. This new process is the *Language of Light*. The Language of Light is a spiritual term used for a natural, spiritual evolutionary process that will take place on Earth. This process will catch us up to speed with those in the afterlife, who already have this ability. At that time on Earth, there will be a new method of communication between individuals. It will replace verbal communication. Others will read your every thought.

I personally, have already been experiencing this in my everyday life. I often communicate in this manner when I am in a highly spiritual state of consciousness and when visiting with the Messengers. I have seen this ability increase with me as I continue to spend time with these God-like Beings.

After writing about my NDE just now, I started to question it. Did I really die? Was this some kind of experience to show me what takes place when a human dies? Was it a healing or all of those things? If I were actually dead, why would I go into a casket in a movie? Wouldn't I just go to a heavenly place and talk to a Being who would have a discussion with me as some others have done during an NDE? I have no answers to all of these questions at the moment, but what I do know beyond a shadow of a doubt is that the experience taught me what it's like to die.

My NDE was very real for me and for my husband as well. I also know beyond a shadow of a doubt that there is life after death because of my visits with friends and family who are now living in a spirit world after their deaths.

My immediate family and several relatives have had many supernatural experiences similar to mine during their Earth lifetimes. My mother was one of those people. She had discussed many of them with me in earlier years, before her death.

In her lifetime, she also experienced what it was like to be involved with several churches that were very dogmatic. She was very religious and concerned for my safety because of my belief in so many so-called supernatural events.

She knew that I believed in God as the highest power. She acknowledged that I lived a very spiritual life and was always the most caring person when it came to the needs of others. She still had some concerns that the spiritual events I viewed as positive might actually be negative and someday turn on me. She eventually learned that my guidance was pure and that I would be just fine when it was time for me to leave this Earth.

She also experienced several miracles in her life. I think her most important miracles were her visits with Jesus. She had a visit with Him early in her life and several visits near her death. The first visit was when she asked people at her church to pray for her. She had smoked cigarettes since she was in her teens and had not been able to stop that bad habit. A short time after her prayer request, she sat in the living room and embroidered. She looked up just as Jesus appeared in full-body form right in front of her. He reached out to her. She thought He wanted her to go with Him.

Her habit took over instead of her instincts. She looked at His outstretched arm and said, "Wait until I get my cigarettes." She reached for them on the table beside her as she got up to go with Him. He vanished right before her eyes. She felt very sad about the way it all transpired, but her cigarette habit was broken forever.

Many years later, she developed an illness that became terminal. Her doctor told her she had six months to live. She only lived about a month or so after she reached that stage of her illness. Though she was gravely ill, she still had a very sharp mind, which amazed all of us. Sometimes she was more alert than any of us, and then there were times when she appeared to be totally absent from her body. During that time period, her transition took many twists and turns.

Several times, we thought she had made her final departure, but she always came back to share whom she had visited with in Heaven; these visits were with Jesus and people she had known in her lifetime. She was not through with the things that she needed to clear up on Earth. She had to make these visits to Heaven before she was ready to allow her body to shut down completely.

When she was actually ready to make her final departure, she returned from another visit to Heaven to finalize things with her immediate family. She came back to tell us about her latest visit with Jesus and to say goodbye to us. She was finally prepared to leave her body after this last visit with Him.

She asked that the immediate family members line up on either side of the bed. She even gave us the specific order of the lineup. At that point, she said she wanted to give each of us a final message.

I was the last one she gave a message to. She asked me to come closer for my message in private. She spoke clearly in my ear as she told me she had just talked to Jesus. She said He told her that He knew who I was and that all was well with me. He also told her that He would be coming to take me when He was ready for me.

Prior to that visit with Jesus, she had had such a hard time leaving her body because she thought she had failed in her job as a mother. She was disturbed that all of her children did not attend church as regularly as she did. She wanted to be sure that we would make it into Heaven when our time came.

Some of her concerns about me were due to my metaphysical/spiritual studies. She also knew a little about my encounters with Beings in spacecraft, and I think this was what worried her the most. She didn't understand it. Over the years, she was never radical about any of those issues. She never mentioned it to me unless I brought the subject up. I guess it was just a motherly instinct to protect her children. She knew that spiritual encounters of all sorts could take place because of her own experiences, but she felt that her experiences were positive because she had that spiritual feeling that came with them. She also felt that she had protection because church was a big part of her life. Thank God she was able to talk to Jesus about me before her passing. To go peacefully, she needed to know that I was on the right path with my life.

After Mom's last goodbye to everyone, she was finally able to pass on. It took her approximately two weeks from the time she started shutting down to the time when she left her body permanently. I was very concerned that she took so much time because of the amount of pain she had.

The day she died, I had called the private nurse to come to her home, because I felt the time was getting near. I wanted to verbally assure her that everything would be all right, and I wanted her to go on without worry. I went into her room and told her that I loved her very much, that all was well with the whole family, and that she had done her job perfectly. I told her that I couldn't stand for her to be in so much pain and that this was my last goodbye and she should go on. When I spoke to her, she didn't seem to be in her body, but I knew she could hear me. The minute I finished talking to her, she raised her pointer finger as a gesture to signal that she got the message.

I heard the door open then; it was the nurse. She entered the room and asked me to turn on another light so she could see a little better. I turned my back to flip the light switch just as my mother took her last breath. She had finally accepted that her work on Earth was done.

A few years after my mother's death, I received a message from her through a psychic medium. I had learned from metaphysical classes that a medium, sometimes called a reader or psychic, is a person who has the gift of communicating with so-called dead people.

One morning as I got out of bed and walked across the room, I heard a voice speak to me telepathically. I heard the words loudly and clearly, "Go to Cassadaga." I had no idea why I was to go there, but I immediately made plans to. When I arrived in Cassadaga, I still didn't know why I was there. I felt like I was on a treasure hunt and waiting for my first clue. The first thing I saw was a bookstore. I went in to see what they had to offer and to possibly find a couple of treasures while I was at it.

Right away, I noticed a bulletin board that had the business cards of mediums displayed on it. I picked a card that I felt drawn to and stuck it in my pocket. I still waited for a clue as to why I was there. Since I had not yet received any specific instructions, I thought maybe I was supposed to go there for relaxation in that peaceful community. Maybe I was just supposed to have lunch at a relaxing restaurant instead of my usual, hectic workday.

I proceeded to a restaurant in the hotel to have lunch. As I sat there, I felt drawn to the business card of the medium again. I pulled it out and gave her a call. She was available in a couple of hours, so I made an appointment with her as it was the strongest feeling that I had had so far as to the purpose of the trip. I always enjoyed a good reading anyway.

After a leisurely lunch, I went to my appointment still not knowing if it was my purpose in Cassadaga. The reading was not very long, but as things turned out, it was very meaningful.

The medium started the reading by saying that my mother was speaking to her and that she had some important information for me. My mother told her that she finally understood the meaning of the metaphysical/spiritual teachings that I had been studying for years. She went on to say that it was very important for me to continue to learn as much here on Earth about these studies as possible. She wanted me to continue on that path to speed up my level of spiritual evolution before I left Earth.

This medium could not have known anything about my lifetime of discussions with my mother regarding this matter, nor about my beliefs, other than that I must have believed in psychic mediums. There were other meaningful messages for me from my mother that day as well, including ones for my daughter regarding health issues.

On my way home, I called my daughter to tell her what had happened. She told me that she had received a visit from my mother that day as well. She was surprised to found out that the visit occurred around the same time as my appointment with the medium. My daughter remembered the time of day because she was not feeling well and had gone to bed to meditate on her health and ask for healing. After I gave her the message from my mother, she was amazed. It was the same exact message she had received that afternoon from her.

A few years after that visit to Cassadaga, my mother paid a personal visit to me in my home one early morning. It was a total surprise to me. I didn't think my mother believed that there was instant, new life in a spirit world after death. I knew she had previously communicated with people on the other side, but she had also been taught in church that she would lie in a grave after her death until the day Jesus returned to Earth. I heard her talking about that one day, and she seemed to believe it.

As I said, I was shocked by her visit because my logic told me that if she didn't believe in life after death in the manner that I did, then she might not know that she could communicate with me from the other side. This visit occurred shortly after the major tragedy in New York on September 11, 2001. Just as I woke up, she appeared and spoke to me telepathically. She said, "You were right about all of the things you tried to tell me regarding God and life after death. I wish I had listened to you and learned more about all of those types of things while I was still living."

She went on to say, "I am currently stuck in a place where I have to study all of the same spiritual teachings that you tried to tell me about. I cannot move forward in spirit until I learn all of it and have a better understanding of how spiritual evolution works. I am now anxious to move forward quickly with this process."

I then asked her if that place had a name. She replied, "I don't know the name of it; I just got here, but it must be New Orleans from the way I am sweating." Her comment was said with humor; it was hysterical to me. After I gave it a good laugh, she continued, "I was transferred because so many people came in all at once. It was overcrowded so they had to move me to this new place."

You had to know my mother and her sense of humor for that to be funny. She always had something humorous to say about everything. What was also funny to me was that she used New Orleans as the description for her current location. My mother had never been to New Orleans, let alone interested in going there. I guess she had pictured it as the hottest, steamiest place she could imagine, or she had heard someone else say that. She did love Florida and the Florida beaches, so she did know what steamy was all about, but she also knew that there was usually a good breeze there.

Because of her visit to me that particular morning, I knew beyond a shadow of a doubt that she was aware that the metaphysical teachings I told her were true. I felt comforted by that, since it was such a concern for her on Earth.

I later had one of those Aha! moments as I realized what she had to say that morning made perfect sense. Her visit occurred right after 9-11. She was transferred right after 9-11, which was why so many people came into spirit world all at once. She made no mention of that day, so I assumed that she knew that I would automatically know it was due to 9-11. It took me a while, but reality finally hit me.

Her early morning visit was very important to me in many ways. I felt good about where she was, and she sounded very happy as she joked with me, just like her normal self. She was no longer in pain and sorrow from earthly matters. After her visit ended, I missed her but knew that she had to move forward with her own spiritual evolution and that I would see her again.

Mom's visit also validated what I believed in spiritually. It was just another way for her to let me know that she now knew I was right about the teachings. It reminded me of the time when she was near death. Jesus had told her that He would be coming to take me when He was ready for me. Nasha had also told me that my People from Rising Star would be coming to take me home. Jesus didn't say anything about me dying. Are these two messages actually one message? It certainly gives me something to ponder; after all, Jesus was visited by His People on the night of his birth as well.

As you know, I had also received a telepathic message from my People that They were coming to take me with Them in Their craft. That particular message was prior to when They did take me into Their craft, so now I still wonder if They were talking about that event or if They will be taking me again in the future. I know that They would take me again, if there was a time when being on this planet would not be safe for me. So many unknowns and so many things to ponder while waiting for answers from my People.

Again, I don't rule out anything in the bizarre world I live in. I can't emphasize enough that everything is not always as it seems. We always need to think outside the box to get true answers. We are so programmed to think that we will leave Earth by death, but…what if the possibility exists that we may at some point leave Earth by a spacecraft instead of death? That's definitely something everyone should ponder.

Chapter 16
Life Before Birth

My mother's visits with me after her so-called death and the visits from other family members and friends after their so-called deaths have taught me a lot. One of the valuable things I have learned is that there is a physical life before birth. You will also be convinced of this after you read the details of a few of these visits. Several of my friends and family members still on Earth have also had visits with their loved ones after their deaths. It seems that this is a pretty common event; however, it is usually not discussed publicly. I feel that most people keep this type of visit in the closet for fear of being criticized in our socially conscious society.

My dad was not exempt from this type of spiritual event, though he would never talk about it to anyone except the family. He saw his mother walk through the living room while she was actually on her deathbed in the bedroom and not up walking around. This event occurred about the time that they later found out she had passed on in her sleep.

After my dad's death, he came to pay me a visit. This visit was many long years after his passing. I wasn't sure he would ever pay me a visit considering the length of time since he had passed. I just assumed that he had reincarnated because so many of my visits with others who have passed on have occurred shortly after the passing of that individual. He was most likely tied up with studying and progressing in spirit just like my mother was doing. When he was alive, he didn't have much time to spend with the family or pursuing a spiritual life. He had several occupations at once, which left no time for him to slow down and smell the roses.

His visit to me came early one morning. At first, I didn't realize what was going on. His visit was totally different than my mother's visit. This time, a movie appeared out of thin air and started playing the minute I woke up and opened my eyes. It was as if there was a movie screen in my bedroom and everything else in the room had disappeared.

It is hard to say how long this movie lasted, but it was very lengthy in content. It was long enough that a feature film could be made from all of the things that I saw. The content was educational and had an inspiring message.

An interesting thing about this movie was the way the end of it was shown to me. A television appeared on the big screen that the movie played on. It looked just like the one in my living room. It was as if the big screen disappeared and the rest of the movie was shown to me on this television that had appeared. At that point, my dad appeared on the television screen just long enough for him to deliver the last few sentences of the movie. Needless to say, I was quite amazed with what had transpired.

This movie was filled with detailed events that played out over a number of years. It told what my dad learned about his life on Earth in hindsight, as seen from the afterlife. You know what they say about hindsight.

It was a great film and a moving story. It was also very unique in the way it had been plotted. There is nothing like a surprise movie in your bedroom when you wake up in the morning. Early mornings, before I get out of bed, are about the only times that my attention can be captured long enough to watch an event like this.

Only my dad would want to portray these events to me to get his message across. The message was a powerful one that applies to everyone and one that I needed to see as well.

After the movie was over, I knew that I was supposed to have the story produced for the public. Since the last part of it was shown on the television screen, it seemed that it might be an omen to say it should be shown on television in the future. The best reason for that might be that more people would be able to see it than in a theater. It was too long and detailed for a one-time television show, though, but could possibly work as a miniseries; or a full-length movie would do it justice. The important thing is that the message should get out there. It will help others with their lives' paths and their lives after death.

As I've mentioned before, I always keep a tape recorder and notebook nearby because of the huge number of events happening in my life. I could never remember all of these details without my trusty notes and recordings. Thank goodness, I had fresh batteries on this particular morning considering the lengthy details of the movie. This movie is still on my list of things to do, as are all of the things I have been asked to do.

Another special visit that I had with someone on the other side was with my grandmother. That visit was several years after she passed on as well. That time I actually paid the visit to her at her present location, but not by my own doing or thoughts. I ended up there without notice. It was as if I was transported into another physical realm of existence.

I found myself standing inside the doorway of a room that was filled with people. They were all dressed as if this was a semiformal occasion that I had popped in on. It reminded me of a modern-day cocktail party. People milled around and talked in groups.

I didn't recognize anyone and wondered why I was there with all of these strangers. I turned to look at two men that stood in the middle of the room; both wore well-tailored, dark suits. On the far side of the room, I saw a group of ladies sitting on a sofa. I immediately focused on one specific lady who appeared to be about forty-five-years old. I thought she looked familiar, but I couldn't figure out how I knew her. As our eyes met, she gave me a big smile. At that point, I knew that she was my grandmother on my mother's side of the family.

I didn't recognize her right away, because she looked so much younger than I would have expected her to. She was in her early sixties at the time of her death. I had seen pictures of her when she was around the age of forty-five, and she looked very much like she did in those pictures.

The entire event was different from the other visits I had experienced in the past. As I have said before, with the kind of life I live, I never know what to expect. I guess the fact that each event is different actually makes it more believable for me. It allows me to know beyond a shadow of a doubt that the experiences are real.

Then there was the visit with my dear friend, Tom. Tom had passed away at the early age of thirty-eight. He and his ex-wife were both friends of mine. The way I met those two is another really long, uncanny story in itself.

Tom became seriously ill with no warning. He was hospitalized and never recovered. I got a phone call from Peggy, his ex-wife, to tell me that he had passed away. Shortly afterward, he came to me at my home. He said, "Please come to see me at the funeral home; bring only one white rose and place it across my chest. I don't want a lot of flowers. I did not want to be viewed at a funeral home, either; I wanted to be cremated."

I told Peggy about the things Tom had told me. I explained that he wanted to be cremated. She gasped and looked as though she was in utter shock. She was very upset because she had already made all of the arrangements for him at the funeral home. There was to be no cremation. It was too late to change anything.

All of a sudden, she recalled that when he was sick he had told her that he wanted to be cremated if he died. He had also told her that he wanted his ashes sprinkled at sea. He had served in the US Navy when he was younger. I asked her why she had not granted his wish. She said that she thought he was just talking out of his head due to being so ill and on so many drugs for pain. She went on to tell me that he had also come to her after his death to give her a similar message. He told her to bring only one red rose and lay it across his chest.

A year or so after Tom died, I had been traveling and was really tired. I got home in the middle of the afternoon and took my suitcase straight to the bedroom. I sat on the edge of the bed and threw my body backward to collapse for a few minutes. As I hit the bed, I recall staring at the ceiling for a second, then I quickly zoomed out of my body. I went directly to a beautiful, peaceful city where I met eye-to-eye with Tom.

I could feel myself standing on a sidewalk as I spotted him at a distance. He walked down the sidewalk and straight toward me. I didn't see any other people there on the street. The place looked similar in structure to cities that we have here on Earth, but it didn't feel or look the same otherwise. The buildings were very tall and seemingly endless. They all seemed to be touching each other or were just very close together like apartment buildings. It looked like a very big city with streets and normal- to wider-sized sidewalks. I got the sense that there were no motorized vehicles there.

Everything, including the sidewalks and buildings, was a soft, pale-beige color. There was a brilliant white light that shined from above and all around. It seemed as though everything was touched by this white light. It was as if there was a haze or mist that was evenly distributed in the background and in the air. I could see everything very clearly, even though the white rays were shining brightly in, on, and around everything, including Tom. The light was so intense that I was amazed it didn't hurt my eyes.

I just stood there on the sidewalk mesmerized by all I saw. I looked ahead of me and saw that Tom was very near me by that time. At first, I didn't think he saw me standing there because he was looking down at the sidewalk, as if to watch his step. As he came closer, he looked me straight in the eye, and he gave me his familiar, big smile. He was always such a happy, carefree person. He seemed to enjoy every minute of life.

There he was in spirit, looking exactly the way he did when he was healthy. The only difference was that his deep smile-lines had disappeared, which made him look younger. As he smiled, I could see that he still had the same, crooked, front tooth that he had when he was alive.

He wore a loose, white shirt like hippies used to wear. It hung about ten inches below the waistline and flowed in the breeze. He also wore sandals and a pair of white, loose-fitting pants.

He always had shoulder-length, blond hair that was slightly receding. Yes, he still had that same blonde hair, styled the same way but without the receding hairline. His hair gently blew in the breeze with the brilliant, white light shining through it, causing it to glow and sparkle.

I headed toward him to give him a hug when suddenly, I found myself back in my bedroom, still lying there on the bed and looking up at the ceiling. I had returned to my bedroom as quickly as I left it. What a neat experience. Another interesting thing about that experience was that it occurred after I had just returned from a place that he loved. While I was on that trip, I had sensed his presence there with me as well.

After the fact, I had to laugh about seeing Tom in that hippie-looking shirt, because Tom was a bit of a hippie in his earthly life. The sandals and shirt were definitely something that he wore in life here. Who says, "You can't take it with you"? He definitely looked like he was comfortable, happy, and walked with a purpose.

I wondered if had I accidently wandered or floated into his space or reality…or if he created that event. Knowing Tom, I would have to say he created it. He had a way of making things happen. We were just friends, but we had a special spiritual connection.

Years later, I saw Peggy. She had remarried and had a new baby. As I held her baby girl, I could sense that this baby was different. She had an aura of energy around her that made her feel like an angel. I had never had that kind of feeling with a baby before. She was glowing and felt weightless, as if she was floating. That was a very unusual experience for me. I have never again experienced an aura of energy around a living person that was like the one about this baby, except for the one around a man that I met years later. His name is Paul, a dear friend of mine. Being around Paul's pure energy is like being with a human that is half angel. I feel very balanced and calm around him.

During my visit with Peggy, I remembered that I had previously had a premonition that Tom was going to reincarnate and come back to her. When I told her about this, she looked surprised. She told me that she had had the same premonition. I guess she realizes now that Tom would stop at nothing to get back to her, even coming back as a girl to win her love.

We definitely never lose touch with friends and family when they go into spirit. They are never far away. This I know beyond a shadow of a doubt. Each experience with them that I have had is unique, but the reality still remains the same. My next visit was just as unique as the others and very special as well.

When my stepfather passed away, I was not feeling well enough to fly up north for his funeral, much to my regret. He didn't let that stop him from creating an experience for me. Miracles will never cease in my life, thank God and my other miracle-working friends.

One morning, not too long after he died, I awoke to an unusual event. I did my morning stretches and then sat up to get out of bed. Before I could, I found myself at a funeral. It was my stepfather's funeral.

I stood near the casket but never looked in it, which seemed odd to me after the fact. There were a lot of family members there standing around and talking to me. The stranger thing was that the people I talked with as I stood by the casket were people that were not able to attend his funeral either.

After a while, I decided to leave the building by myself. I walked down a long sidewalk that met up with another set of steps that went into a huge cathedral. When I got to the end of the steps, I looked over at the cathedral and saw my stepfather standing there in front of these huge doors. He looked much more youthful than when he was alive. He just stood there all by himself. He was dressed handsomely in a designer outfit. It consisted of a black suit, black shoes, a white shirt, and a black- and white-patterned tie to match.

I recall saying a strange thing to him, "Why aren't you at the funeral?" He replied, "I went to this door and nobody was there." I told him that he had gone to the wrong door and that I would walk him over to the correct building.

I had spent a lot of time with him in the recent past and knew how feeble he was getting. I put my arm around him to stabilize him as we walked. I soon realized that he didn't need stabilizing. He was as strong and sturdy as a body builder, much to my amazement.

As we reached the door of the building where the casket was located, he stopped and said, "I wanted to make sure that you were able to be at my funeral." Then I vanished from his side and was back on my bed in a sitting position.

He created all of this for me so that I could be at his funeral. After his death, he obviously knew that I had wished I could be there for him. The visit that he created fulfilled his wish as well as mine.

After this experience, I found it interesting that I knew I was at his funeral, yet I still asked him why he wasn't at the funeral himself. I can see now that the whole experience was created in that manner for everything to flow as it did. There is a lot behind this thought that I can't put into words; hopefully, it comes across with the same meaning that I feel about it.

The very next morning after my visit with my stepfather, I awoke to another visitor from the other side. I was with my Aunt Pam who is also in spirit. She looked half the age that she was when she died. Just then, the phone rang, and I slammed back into my body and didn't get to visit with her.

I thought it was interesting that Aunt Pam's visit came the day after my stepfather's, as they were not blood relatives but were related through marriage. She was my mom's half sister. I felt that it was no coincidence that both visits occurred near the same time. It was as if family members, as a group, had focused in on me at that time and that all of it had been orchestrated in the same manner. These visits with family and friends have brought me more proof, and I now know beyond a shadow of a doubt that life goes on after death. With all of this proof, how can I deny that fact? I also sense that we are with family and friends even after we pass on. I have seen and told you about some of my past lives with the same immediate family members that I have had in this lifetime.

My experiences with those from the other side are not limited to family and friends as you know by now. I was about to experience another unique visit that was truly out of the norm, even for me. I would even put it in the miraculous category—not that the others were not miraculous, but I find it hard to categorize this event. All I can say is that even I could not believe my eyes this time.

I had gone down to the southeastern coast of Florida to visit a friend whose business is on the ocean. We had a long lunch at an ocean-side restaurant before I left to head back home. I felt a strong, positive energy in the air as I drove back north along the ocean road. It was very relaxing and peaceful as I drove in my customized van. With the large, front window on this type of vehicle, I had a great view of what was ahead of and above me.

As I drove along, out of the blue, I heard a voice in my head say, "Look up." I immediately looked up at the sky and out over the ocean. My eyes were wide open, and they suddenly fixed on a sight. I was afraid to blink for fear of missing something. I was looking at a woman's face in the sky. My first thought was "What the?!" No, I wasn't drunk or hallucinating. Her head and face covered the entire sky in front of me.

Her face was alive, and she looked back at me. Her expression was frozen for a second. All of a sudden, she burst into a wide smile as our eyes met.

Her face was as clear as any photograph, yet it was alive; it was definitely as alive as you and me. The head and face were not a cloud in the shape of a head. It was a real face superimposed over the sky.

I know; I keep using the word *alive* and driving the point home, but she was alive. How could that be? When I write about it, I can't help but express how shocking it was. Again, I could barely believe my own eyes, but that was exactly what happened. It certainly left nothing to the imagination. I know that it's impossible for it to have happened, but it did.

I was really lucky that I didn't have a wreck. Time stood still for me. When it was over and the face had disappeared, I found myself still driving along the ocean-side road. I had not stopped the van.

I could not give this female face a name because it was not a face that I recognized. I was not shown in any way shape or form who she was; it is still a mystery. However, my feeling is that my People from Rising Star had something to do with this event. I would like to believe that she was Mother Mary and that she paid a visit to me for all the good deeds that I had done. However, I would not be that egotistical as to presume such a thing.

Many claim that they have had experiences similar to mine but that theirs were, in fact, with Mother Mary. I do not doubt them at all. I could make all kinds of wild claims about my experience with that face, but I just don't know for sure.

Just prior to that experience, there was a lady in Georgia who experienced actual events with Mother Mary on a regular basis. She offered weekly meetings to the public to bring forth messages from Mother Mary. I once spoke with another woman who actually went to Georgia for one of those meetings. She did experience a miracle in her life at that time and witnessed another lady's silver rosary turn to gold. I mention this because years ago, my People asked me to take Their messages public in the same manner as this lady was doing. That was around 1992 or 1993, right before I met Doctor Mack. At that time, my People were more active with me than normal.

I did not follow through with Their request to go public in that exact manner, because I didn't have the nerve to be that public. I wasn't as brave as she was and I didn't know as much as I do now about my People, the Messengers. In some way, I regret that I didn't do more public work like she did, but I did finally do quite a bit of work that made up for it and I am not done yet.

I know beyond a shadow of a doubt that a whole new reality has been unveiled for me by these Messengers, a new reality that is a truth that resonates with my soul. It has given me a firm, spiritual foundation that has created a whole new meaning for life.

I have also learned that not only is there life on other stars and planets in the Universe, but there is God, the highest power or frequency who rules this Universe.

We Earthlings and the so-called aliens coexist in God's Universe with Jesus and the Holy Spirit. We all have a soul, which is also known as a spirit. We are all energy but on different levels or frequencies than that of Jesus and the Holy Spirit.

In our Bible, the Holy Spirit is described only as the Holy Spirit, without another name that I am aware of, but He has a soul just as Jesus does. All souls exist in heavenly places until they incarnate into a body. We are all one and the same, coexisting in the same Universe.

Heaven is just a location in the Universe, another dimension of reality or plane of existence. There are many levels of Heaven, so in a sense, you could say that there are many Heavens. This conjures up the possibility that Heaven may be on another planet. It is definitely a tangible place.

A lot of people on Earth believe that we are the only life-form in God's Universe and claim superiority, in a sense. If you recall, I told you earlier in this book that I had been informed by the Light Beings that They are not aliens but Brothers of Man as well as Messengers from God. We are all brothers and sisters, we are all one and the same, and we are certainly not alone in this Universe.

As you know, I have been instructed by my People to write this book for the purpose of giving people faith. This book and this chapter will have some impact on the faith of those who are open-minded enough to think outside the box.

I have always had faith that life was endless and that life after death exists on many different planes of existence. At this point, my belief is no longer faith based but is now a *matter of fact* for me. I now know beyond a shadow of a doubt that you can never die—you just take on another body elsewhere—death is never final, and our souls live on…and on…and on…

Manufactured by Amazon.ca
Bolton, ON